D1624488

A Christmas Sourcebook

Also in this series:

AN ADVENT SOURCEBOOK
A TRIDUUM SOURCEBOOK
AN EASTER SOURCEBOOK

A CHRISTMAS
SOURCEBOOK

Edited by
Mary Ann Simcoe

Liturgy
Training
Publications
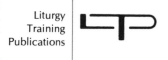

Acknowledgments

This selections in this book are from numerous sources; we are grateful to their publishers and authors for permission to include them. Every effort has been made to determine the ownership of all texts and to make proper arrangements for their use. Any oversight that may have occurred, if brought to our attention, will gladly be corrected in future editions.

Acknowledgments for sources not listed below are in the endnotes.

Excerpts from the English translation of the *Lectionary for Mass* © 1969, International Committee on English in the Liturgy, Inc. (ICEL); excerpts from the English translation of Morning, Evening and the Office of Readings from *The Liturgy of the Hours* © 1974, ICEL; excerpts from *Presidential Prayers for Experimental Use at Mass* © 1983, ICEL. All rights reserved.

Scripture texts used in this work are taken from the *New American Bible* copyright © 1970 and Lectionary for Mass, copyright © 1970 by the Confraternity of Christian Doctrine, Washington DC and are used by license of said copyright owner. No part of the *New American Bible* or *Lectionary for Mass* may be reproduced in any form without permission in writing. All rights reserved.

Page ornaments by Mary Jo Huck.
Series design format by Michael Tapia.

Copyright ©1984, Archdiocese of Chicago. All rights reserved. Liturgy Training Publications, 1800 North Hermitage Avenue, Chicago IL 60622-1101; 312/486-8970.

Printed in the United States of America

ISBN 0-930467-08-6

Contents

Introduction

More than any other days and nights of the year, those of Christmas and Epiphany have stirred human flesh to create, compose, dance and sing about the mystery of God with and for us. Words cannot contain that mystery, yet for two millenia the Christian community has been attempting to speak and sing it in words for worship. *A Christmas Sourcebook* offers some of these texts from the Christmastime liturgy—prayers, poems, hymns and homilies, scripture. Most of the scripture readings and major sacramental texts of the Roman rite are here. The liturgy of the hours has been tapped. There are offerings from the Eastern rites, the Episcopal *Book of Common Prayer* and contemporary writing.

The liturgy is never captured in a book. Liturgy has gestures and processions, vesture and chorus and proclamation all together. Only in these do the words of this book have their true home. Yet even alone on a page these words give us glimpses of the depth and richness, not only of the Christmastime ritual tradition, but of the mystery itself.

The arrangement of the material is somewhat chronological. We begin with the Christmas Vigil and progress through the days to the Baptism of the Lord, but the ideas and realities which these words clothe are far from tidy themes. Wonderful threads of the Christmas-Epiphany mystery distinguish themselves: the renewal and rejoicing of creation; the favor of God; the *Hodie*, or Today, which the church ever sings to claim the mystery in this time; the intermingling of divinity and humanity; the light which conquers darkness; the manifestation of the cross and salvation in the telling of the birth. These are a few. No one of them dominates any of the festival days.

And so, the progression of passages in this sourcebook does not isolate any of these threads, but intertwines them as does the liturgy. Like a fugue with each of its melodies playing over and through the others, the "themes" of the Christmastime liturgy are repeated and developed.

This book came to be by the gracious assistance of many who offered who offered suggestions for the texts to be included: Peter Scagnelli, Sam Mackintosh, Mary McGann, RSCJ, Richard Proulx, Father Chrysogonus, OCSO, David Hermann, Gordon Lathrop, Christopher Fairman, Gabe Huck. Thanks to them!

Tradition, it is said, is that part of a people's history which is still living. During this time when our culture so resists and seems to crush the keeping of the days of Christmas-Epiphanytime, may this collection offer encouragement to let our tradition live—in liturgy, at home, in preaching and prayer—in us.

Mary Ann Simcoe

WOLCUM be thou hevene king,
Wolcom, born in one morning,
Wolcum for whom we sall sing!
Wolcum Yole!

Wolcum be ye, good Newe Yere,
Wolcum, Twelfthe Day both in fere,
Wolcum sentes lefe and dere,
Wolcum Yole!

Wolcum be ye Candelmesse,
Wolcum be ye Quene of bliss,
Wolcum bothe to more and lesse.
Wolcum Yole!

Wolcum be ye that are here,
Wolcum alle and make good cheer.
Wolcum alle another yere.
Wolcum Yole! *Anonymous*

SOME say, that ever 'gainst that season comes
Wherein our Savior's birth is celebrated,
The bird of dawning singeth all night long:
And then, they say, no spirit dare stir abroad;
The nights are wholesome; then no planets strike,
No fairy takes, nor witch hath power to charm;   *Shakespeare*
So hallow'd and so gracious is the time.   *Hamlet*

WE must see the entire winter cycle as a unit, as one grand feast beginning with dawn on the first Sunday of Advent ("It is now the hour for us to rise from sleep"), growing in brilliance like the sun at Christmas, reaching zenith at Epiphany, and finally setting at Candlemas. It is the glorious symbol of sun and light that gives this season its unity. All is centered on Christ, the true Sun. Christmas really has no date historically, making the symbolism of the winter solstice, *sol invictus*, most appropriate.

Pius Parsch

HOW far Christianity had seized hold of the imagery of the sun-god and appropriated it for her own use can be seen vividly today in the necropolis excavated under St. Peter's in Rome during the search for the apostle's grave. Not far from the traditional site of the tomb there is a small Christian burial chamber of the third century, hemmed in between two pagan mausoleums. The walls of the interior are decorated with biblical themes—fishermen, the Good Shepherd, and Jonah—but in the ceiling there is a splendid mosaic of Helios in his chariot of the sun, drawn by white steeds. His right hand (now lost) must have been raised as a signal for the journey to start. He stands erect, his mantle fluttering in the breeze and his left hand holding the world orb. But it is the nimbus of light rays round his head that reveals his true identity. The lower rays are fashioned into a T cross, a design unknown in earlier pagan examples of this type. The Helios is Christ. No wonder Christian apologists had to deny so often that the members of the church were sun-worshipers!

John Gunstone

THEY call [this day] "the birthday of the unconquered [sun]." But is the sun so unconquered as our Lord who underwent death and overcame it? Or they say it is "the birthday of the sun." But is our Lord not the Sun of right- eousness of whom the prophet Malachi said: "For you who fear my name, the sun of righteousness shall rise, with healing in its wings"?

Anonymous
Third century

THE people are quite right, in a way, when they call this birthday of the Lord "the new sun." . . . We gladly accept the name, because at the coming of the savior not only is humankind saved but the very light of the sun is renewed.

Maximus of Turin
Fifth century

IN the liturgy the solstice themes of the *birth* and the appear- ance of the *light* or the *sun* powerfully recur, and are inter- woven with the related themes of our seeing and of the renewal of the earth. . . .

The theme is not the infancy or childhood of Jesus. It is rather that the presence of the man Jesus is the presence of the Light and of the Sun. . . . Just as with the world's solstice, light is celebrated where light seems most threatened. Sol- stice festivity means to encourage the return of the light. Christian liturgy at solstice means to pray for the Light and to celebrate its presence. . . .

The immense popularity of Christmas among us is probably due to the dominance in North America of people whose ethnic origins are in northern latitudes where the solstice is an impressive and still powerful event, as it is in much of North America as well. Most of what has been added to Christmas over the ages can be interpreted as solstice phenomena: feasting and greetings and greens and the light-tree and lights against the darkness and the yule-log and nostalgia for the recovery of old memories and, for us especially, gift-giving and consumer over-spending—all are attempts to secure the return of light and summertime wholeness, are mid-winter protest.

These solstice phenomena are powerful metaphors for us. The darkness does stand for our fears and the feast does awaken—perhaps more than we would have them awakened—our hopes. These metaphors ought not be easily maligned. The pastoral intention of the origin of the feast may be recalled. The human feast of Christmas needs a good deal of sympathetic interpretation and loving support. We have had enough campaigns against the world's Christmas. It is more important to ask: "Why do we keep it with such vigor?" For us solstice is an immensely important human and therefore pastoral occasion.

Gordon Lathrop

CHRIST is the Morning Star,
who, when the night of this world is past,
gives to his saints the promise of the light of life,
and opens everlasting day.

Venerable Bede
Eighth century

A DAM lay in bondage,
Bounded in a bond;
Four thousand winters
Thought he not too long.
And all was for an apple,
An apple that he took,
As holy men find written
In their book.

Had not the apple taken been,
The apple taken been,
Then never would our Lady
been heaven's queen.
Blessed be the time
That apple taken was,
Therefore may we sing it,
Deo gratias, Deo gratias,
Deo gratias, Deo gratias.

Anonymous
Fifteenth century

W E know from our study of primitive cultures that trees
remaining green in the winter have long suggested
special godlike powers. . . . As Christianity supplanted older,
pagan religions, the decorating of evergreens continued in
various parts of northern Europe on many special occasions. . . .
The Roman Catholic church frequently banned or otherwise
tried to discourage the use of the evergreen, but the age-
old custom remained so deeply ingrained in the German
culture that the tree eventually became transformed into a
Christian symbol.

Although the veneration of the evergreen is firmly rooted in pre-Christian traditions, the Christmas tree has two interesting Christian traditions behind it. During the fourteenth and fifteenth centuries evergreens with apples hung from their boughs were known to have played an important role in the miracle plays presented in or outside churches on the twenty-fourth of December. . . . In the early church calendar of saints December 24 was Adam and Eve's Day, the occasion for a play depicting the dramatic events concerning the fruit tree in the Garden of Eden. In many cities, before the performance the actors paraded through the streets with the actor who would portray Adam carrying the "Paradise tree." In place of the winter-bare branches of a real apple tree, an evergreen decorated with apples was the usual substitute. Since this tree was the only prop on the stage during the play, the image left a lasting impression associated with Christmas long after the medieval plays were no longer performed. By the seventeenth century evergreens hung with apples were no longer considered strictly trees of temptation and were traditionally decorated each Christmas, though as late as the latter part of the nineteenth century people in northern Germany still bought little figures of Adam and Eve and the serpent to put under their "Tree of Life."

The Christmas tree also has Christian associations as old as the tenth century that link it to flowering or fruit-bearing trees rather than to the evergreen. Throughout Europe there are records and folk tales concerning trees and bushes that mysteriously burst into bloom on Christmas Eve or Day. Beginning in the sixteenth century references indicate that many Germans cut cherry and other flowering branches and took them into their homes on St. Andrew's Day (November 30). The branches were put in water in a warm room and "forced" in the hope of obtaining blooms in time for Christmas.

The oldest Christmas tree to be decorated standing in a parlor as we know the tradition today is described in a fragment of a 1605 travel diary left us by an unidentified visitor to Strasbourg. The writer tells of fir trees set up and hung with paper roses of many different colors and with apples, flat wafers, gilded candies, and sugar. In early Christian art the rose was a symbol for the Virgin Mary, and the flat wafers are obviously related to the "host," the communion symbol for Christ. A tree decorated with such wafers or cookies with religious designs became known as a *Christbaum*. By the seventeenth century, then, the age-old, winter-defying evergreen was a common sight in Christian homes honoring the Christ Child each Christmas.

Phillip V. Snyder

R EJOICE, Jerusalem! All you lovers of Sion, share our festivities! On this day the age-old bonds of Adam's condemnation were broken, paradise was opened for us, the serpent was crushed, and the woman, whom he once deceived, lives now as mother of the creator. . . . Let all creation dance and thrill with joy, for Christ has come to call it home and to save our souls.

Processional antiphon
Vigil of Christmas
Byzantine rite

THEY (the Copts) keep vigil from the evening of the night before the Nativity and have the custom of lighting a very large number of lights in their churches and decorating them. In Egypt this feast is celebrated on the 29th day of the month of Kohiak. Till now, it has remained one of the most solemn feasts of the year. Under the Fatimites, Cairo pastries, cakes made from flour, others of julep, dishes of fritters, and of the fish known as mullet, were served to high dignitaries, great stewards, emirs with collar of office, secretaries and others. The fire game is a custom of the Christians on the day of the Nativity. . . . We have witnessed Christmas in Cairo, Misr, and throughout Egypt become an occasion of magnificent solemnity. Candles decorated with pretty colors and delightful images were sold for considerable sums. No one, however high or low his station, failed to buy some for his children and family. These lights were called *faounis, fanous* in the singular. The stalls in the bazaars were hung with great quantities of them, of considerable beauty. There was a veritable fever to bump their prices up, to the extent that I have seen one originally priced at a thousand or perhaps five hundred silver *dirhems* rise to more than seventy gold *mithqal*. Even the beggars in the streets took part in these festivities: they prayed to God to be given a *fanous*, and people bought them little tapers worth a *dirhem* or so. Later the Egyptian troubles that caused so many luxurious customs to disappear, ruined the Christmas *fanous* trade, of which little tract remains.

Fifteenth century

U NDERLYING all festive joy kindled by a specific circumstance there has to be an absolutely universal affirmation
extending to the world as a whole, to the reality of things and
the existence of humanity itself. Naturally, this approval need
not be a product of conscious reflection; it need not be formu-
lated at all. Nevertheless, it remains the sole foundation for
festivity, no matter what happens to be celebrated *in con-
creto*. And as the radical nature of negation deepens, and
consequently as anything but ultimate arguments becomes
ineffectual, it becomes more necessary to refer to this ultimate
foundation. By ultimate foundation I mean the conviction that
the prime festive occasion, which alone can ultimately justify
all celebration, really exists; that, to reduce it to the most con-
cise phrase, at bottom *everything that is, is good, and it is good
to exist*. For we cannot have the experience of receiving what
is loved, unless the world and existence as a whole represent
something good and therefore beloved to us.

Josef Pieper
In Tune with the World

T OMORROW the wickedness of the earth will be
destroyed, and the savior of the world will rule over us.

Office of Readings
Roman rite

O F course you can't help thinking of my being in prison over Christmas, and it is bound to throw a shadow over the few hours of happiness which still await you in these times. All I can do to help is to assure you that I know you will keep it in the same spirit as I do, for we are agreed on how Christmas ought to be kept. How could it be otherwise when my attitude to Christmas is a heritage I owe to you? I need not tell you how much I long to be released and to see you all again. But for years you have given us such lovely Christmasses, that our grateful memories are strong enough to cast their rays over a darker one. In times like these we learn as never before what it means to possess a past and a spiritual heritage untrammelled by the changes and chances of the present. A spiritual heritage reaching back for centuries is a wonderful support and comfort in face of all temporary stresses and strains. I believe that the man who is aware of such reserves of power need not be ashamed of the tender feelings evoked by the memory of a rich and noble past, for such feelings belong in my opinion to the better and nobler part of humankind. They will not overwhelm those who hold fast to values of which no one can deprive them.

For a Christian there is nothing peculiarly difficult about Christmas in a prison cell. I daresay it will have more meaning and will be observed with greater sincerity here in this prison than in places where all that survives of the feast is its name. That misery, suffering, poverty, loneliness, helplessness and guilt look very different to the eyes of God from what they do to man, that God should come down to the very place which men usually abhor, that Christ was born in a stable because there was no room for him in the inn—these are things which a prisoner can understand better than anyone else. For the prisoner the Christmas story is glad tidings in a very real sense. And that faith gives the prisoner a part in the communion of saints, a fellowship transcending the bounds of time and space and reducing the months of confinement here to insignificance.

On Christmas Eve I shall be thinking of you all very much, and I want you to believe that I too shall have a few hours of real joy and that I am not allowing my troubles to get the better of me. . . .

It will certainly be a quiet Christmas for everybody, and the children will look back on it for long afterwards. But for the first time, perhaps, many will learn the true meaning of Christmas.

Dietrich Bonhoeffer
Letter to his parents
December 17, 1943

I have lighted the candles, Mary . . .
How softly breathes your little Son

My wife has spread the table
With our best cloth. There are apples,
Bright as red clocks, upon the mantel.
The snow is a weary face at the window.
How sweetly does He sleep

"Into this bitter world, O Terrible Huntsman!"
I say, and she takes my hand— "Hush,
You will wake Him."

The taste of tears is on her mouth
When I kiss her. I take an apple
And hold it tightly in my fist:
The cold, swollen face of war leans in the window.

They are blowing out the candles, Mary . . .
The world is a thing gone mad tonight.
O hold Him tenderly, dear Mother,
For His is a kingdom in the hearts of men.

"I Have Lighted
the Candles, Mary"
Kenneth Patchen

L IFT up, O gates, your lintels;
reach up, you ancient portals,
that the king of glory may come in!
Who is this king of glory?
The LORD, strong and mighty,
the LORD, mighty in battle.
Lift up, O gates, your lintels;
reach up, you ancient portals,
that the king of glory may come in!
Who is this king of glory?
The LORD of hosts; he is the king of glory.

From Psalm 24

I N Russia, the custom exists of fasting [on the Christmas vigil] until the first star appears. This brings to mind both the star which led the magi to Bethlehem and Christ who is the true light. May this day also be a day of fast in our souls: let us abstain from all bad or useless thoughts and speech, and await in silence and composure the savior who is coming to us. Darkness falls. Soon the first star will rise and mark, according to the church calendar, the start of the new day and of the great feast of Christmas. With the rising of this star, may the light of our Lord rise for us so that, in the words of the apostle Peter, "Ye do well that ye take heed, as unto a light that shineth in a dark place, until the day dawn, and the day star arise in your hearts."

A monk of the Eastern church

FOR Zion's sake I will not be silent,
for Jerusalem's sake I will not be quiet,
Until her vindication shines forth like the dawn
and her victory like a burning torch.

Nations shall behold your vindication,
and all kings your glory;
You shall be called by a new name
pronounced by the mouth of the Lord.

You shall be a glorious crown in the hand of the Lord,
a royal diadem held by your God.
No more shall men call you "Forsaken,"
or your land "Desolate,"
But you shall be called "My Delight,"
and your land "Espoused."
For the Lord delights in you,
and makes your land his spouse.

As a young man marries a virgin,
your Builder shall marry you;

Isaiah 62:1–5
Vigil of Christmas
Roman rite

And as a bridegroom rejoices in his bride
so shall your God rejoice in you.

I N time it came round, the time
ripe for the birth of a boy.
Much as a bridegroom steps
fresh from the chamber of joy,

arm in arm he arrived
entwining the sweetheart he chose.
Both in a byre at hand
the pleasant mother reposed

among oxen and burros and such
as the winter sky drove in.
How they struck up a tune, those folk!
Sweeter the angels sang!

There was a bridal to chant!
There was a pair well wed!
But why did he sob and sob,
God in his rough-hewn bed?

Such a dazzle of tears!—this gift
all that the bride could bring?
How the mother was struck at so
topsy-turvy a thing:

distress of the flesh, in God!
in man, the pitch of delight!
Pairs never coupled so;
different as day and night.

"Of the Nativity"
John of the Cross

A family record of Jesus Christ, son of David, son of Abraham. Abraham was the father of Isaac, Isaac the father of Jacob, Jacob the father of Judah and his brothers.
Judah was the father of Perez and Zerah,
    whose mother was Tamar.
Perez was the father of Hezron,
Hezron the father of Ram.
Ram was the father of Amminadab,
Amminadab the father of Nahshon,
Nahshon the father of Salmon.
Salmon was the father of Boaz, whose mother was
    Rahab,
Boaz was the father of Obed, whose mother was Ruth.
Obed was the father of Jesse,
Jesse the father of King David.
David was the father of Solomon, whose mother had
    been the wife of Uriah.
Solomon was the father of Rehoboam,
Rehoboam the father of Abijah,
Abijah the father of Asa.
Asa was the father of Jehoshaphat,
Jehoshaphat the father of Joram,
Joram the father of Uzziah.
Uzziah was the father of Jotham,
Jotham the father of Ahaz,
Ahaz the father of Hezekiah.
Hezekiah was the father of Manasseh,
Manasseh the father of Amos,
Amos the father of Josiah.
Josiah became the father of Jechoniah and his brothers at
    the time of the Babylonian exile.
After the Babylonian exile
Jechoniah was the father of Shealtiel,

Shealtiel the father of Zerubbabel.
Zerubbabel was the father of Abiud,
Abiud the father of Eliakim,
Eliakim the father of Azor.
Azor was the father of Zadok,
Zadok the father of Achim,
Achim the father of Eliud.
Eliud was the father of Eleazar,
Eleazar the father of Matthan,
Matthan the father of Jacob.
Jacob was the father of Joseph the husband of Mary.
It was of her that Jesus who is called the Messiah was
    born.
Thus the total number of generations is:
   from Abraham to David, fourteen generations;
   from David to the Babylonian captivity,
      fourteen generations;
   from the Babylonian captivity to the Messiah,
      fourteen generations.

Now this is how the birth of Jesus Christ came about. When his mother Mary was engaged to Joseph, but before they lived together, she was found with child through the power of the Holy Spirit. Joseph her husband, an upright man unwilling to expose her to the law, decided to divorce her quietly. Such was his intention when suddenly the angel of the Lord appeared in a dream and said to him: "Joseph, son of David, have no fear about taking Mary as your wife. It is by the Holy Spirit that she has conceived this child. She is to have a son and you are to name him Jesus because he will save his people from their sins." All this happened to fulfull what the Lord had said through the prophet:

"The virgin shall be with child
and give birth to a son,
and they shall call him Emmanuel,"

a name which means "God is with us." When Joseph awoke
he did as the angel of the Lord had directed him and
received her into his home as his wife. He had no relations
with her at any time before she bore a son, whom he named
Jesus.

Matthew 1:1–25
Vigil of Christmas
Roman rite

THE prodigious expanses of time which preceded the first Christmas were not empty of Christ: they were imbued with the influx of his power. It was the ferment of his conception that stirred up the cosmic masses and directed the initial developments of the biosphere. It was the travail preceding his birth that accelerated the development of instinct and the birth of thought upon the earth. Let us have done with the stupidity which makes a stumbling-block of the endless eras of expectancy imposed on us by the Messiah: the fearful, anonymous labors of primitive man, the beauty fashioned through its age-long history by ancient Egypt, the anxious expectancies of Israel, the patient distilling of the attar of oriental mysticism, the endless refining of wisdom by the Greeks: all these were needed before the Flower could blossom on the rod of Jesse and of all humanity. All these preparatory processes were cosmically and biologically necessary that Christ might set foot upon our human stage. And all this labor was set in motion by the active, creative awakening of his soul inasmuch as that human soul had been chosen to breathe life into the universe. When Christ first appeared . . . in the arms of Mary he had already stirred up the world.

Pierre Teilhard de Chardin

IT is truly a marvelous exchange: the creator . . . , taking a body, gives us his Godhead. The redeemer has come into the world to do this wonderful work. . . . One of us had broken the bond that made us God's children, one of us had to tie it again and pay the ransom. This could not be done by one who came from the old, wild and diseased trunk; a new branch, healthy and noble, had to be grafted into it. He became one of us, more than this, he became one with us. For this is the marvelous thing about the human race, that we are all one. If it were otherwise, if we were all autonomous individuals, living beside each other quite free and independent, the fall of the one could not have resulted in the fall of all. In that case, on the other hand, the ransom might have been paid for and imputed to us, but his justice could not have been passed on to the sinners; no justification would have been possible. But he came to be *one* mysterious Body with us: he our head, we his members.

Edith Stein

THE vigil of Christmas has its own proper solemnity at Prime in the announcement of Christ's birthday. In some European monasteries the chanter, vested in alb and violet cope, steps into the middle of the choir, accompanied by ministers with candles and censer. He incenses the Martyrology on the violet-covered lectern, and after announcing the date begins to sing. All stand with heads uncovered, as at the gospel. At the phrase, "in Bethlehem," all kneel; and at the words, "the birth of our Lord," all prostrate for the first adoration of the Son of God become man. The passage begins with the fixation of the date according to ancient computation:

In the year 5199 since the creation of the world,
    when God made heaven and earth;
in the year 2957 since the flood;
in the year 2015 since Abraham's birth;
in the year 1510 since the exodus of the people of
    Israel from Egypt under the guidance of Moses;
in the year 1032 since David was anointed king;
in the 65th week of years according to Daniel's
    prophecy;
in the 194th Olympiad, in the year 752 after the
    building of Rome;
in the 42nd year of the reign of Octavian Augustus,
    when there was peace in the whole world;
in the 6th era of the world's history;
Jesus Christ, eternal God and Son of the eternal
    Father, desired to sanctify the world by his
    gracious coming.
He was conceived by the Holy Spirit, and now
    after nine months
He is born at Bethlehem in the tribe of Judah
    as man from the virgin Mary.
The birth of our Lord Jesus in the flesh.

Roman Martyrology
Pius Parsch

H AIL King! hail King! blessed is He! blessed is He!
Hail King! hail King! blessed is He! blessed is He!
Hail King! hail King! blessed is He,
 the King of whom we sing,
  All hail! let there be joy!

This night is the eve of the great nativity,
Born is the Son of Mary the Virgin,
The soles of his feet have reached the earth,
The Son of glory down from on high,
Heaven and earth glowed to him,
  All Hail! let there be joy!

The peace of earth to him, the joy of heaven to him,
Behold his feet have reached the world;
The homage of a King be his, the welcome of a Lamb be
 his,
King all victorious, Lamb all glorious,
Earth and ocean illumed to him,
  All hail! let there be joy!

The mountains glowed to him, the plains glowed to
 him,
The voice of the waves with the song of the strand,
Announcing to us that Christ is born,
Son of the King of kings from the land of salvation;
Shone the sun on the mountains high to him,
  All hail! let there be joy!

Shone to him the earth and sphere together,
God the Lord has opened a Door;
Son of Mary Virgin, hasten thou to help me,
Thou Christ of hope, Thou Door of joy,
Golden Sun of hill and mountain,
  All hail! let there be joy!

Offer to the Being from found to cover,
Include stave and stone and beam;
Offer again both rods and cloth,
Be health to the people therein,
   Hail King! hail King! blessed is He! blessed is He!
   Hail King! hail King! blessed is He! blessed is He!
     Ho, hail! blessed the King!
      Let there be joy!

Blessed the King,
Without beginning, without ending,
To everlasting, to eternity,
    Every generation for aye,
    Ho! hi! let there be joy!   Scottish poem

TODAY the virgin is on her way to the cave where she will
give birth in a manner beyond understanding to the Word
who is, in all eternity. Rejoice, therefore, universe, when you
hear it heralded: with the angels and the shepherds, glorify
him who chose to be seen as a new-born babe, while remain-   Preparation of
                                                                the Nativity
ing God in all eternity.   Orthodox Liturgy

Mass at Midnight
Roman rite

GOOD News and great joy to all the world: Today is born our savior, Christ the Lord.

GOD and Father of Jesus,
on this holy night
you give us your Son,
the Lord of the universe
and the savior of all peoples,
as an infant wrapped in swaddling clothes
and lying in a manger.

In the first moments of his life
you showed us the paradox of your love.

Open us up to the mystery of his powerlessness
and enable us to recognize him
in this plain-spoken word
and simple meal.

This we ask in his name,
he who lives and reigns with you
and the Holy Spirit,
one God, for ever and ever.

Mass at Midnight
Contemporary

WITHERED leaves panic
    Before the knives of wind.
They scurry directionless,
Longing for peace,
Burial in a swansdown of flurries.
Deadblown, yet swirled into false life,
Their nature calls for a return to earth—
To become bits and pieces of the kingdom
From which new life will grow.

Darkness drives down the sun,
Loosing night cold as blue metal;
Together we beg the return of fire
And you hear, O Lord.
Sun's slow revolve enthrones a
Little one on wood warmed with straw.
Childbirth is risky—he comes
As he goes
In a rush of blood and water.
In the night, with loaves and wine,
We become the little one;
Blood brothers and water sisters,
Bits and pieces of the kingdom.

"Leaves in Solstice"
Dennis Kennedy

Of the Father's love begotten
Ere the worlds began to be,
He is Alpha and Omega,
He the source, the ending he,
Of the things that are, that have been,
And that future years shall see,
Evermore and evermore.

Oh, that birth forever blessed,
When the virgin, full of grace,
By the Holy Ghost conceiving,
Bore the savior of our race,
And the babe, the world's redeemer,
First revealed his sacred face,
Evermore and evermore.

This is he whom seers in old time
Chanted of with one accord,
Whom the voices of the prophets
Promised in their faithful word;
Now he shines, the long expected;
Let creation praise its Lord
Evermore and evermore.

Let the heights of heav'n adore him;
Angel hosts, his praises sing;
Pow'rs, dominions, bow before him
And extol our God and King;
Let no tongue on earth be silent,
Ev'ry voice in concert ring
Evermore and evermore.

Christ, to thee, with God the Father,
And, O Holy Ghost, to thee,
Hymn and chant and high thanksgiving
And unwearied praises be:

Honor, glory, and dominion,
And eternal victory
Evermore and evermore! Amen

Prudentius
Fourth century

A T that time, since Mary was of the house of David, she registered with the Venerable Joseph in Bethlehem. She was with child, having conceived virginally. Her time was come and they could find no room in the inn, but the cave seemed a joyful palace for the Queen. Christ is born to renew the likeness that had been lost of old.

Preparation of
the Nativity
Orthodox Liturgy

T HE ruler, the peacemaking ruler, is praised; the whole world has longed for his face.

Evening Prayer I
Roman rite

THE people who walked in darkness
 have seen a great light;
Upon those who dwelt in the land of gloom
 a light has shone.
You have brought them abundant joy
 and great rejoicing,
As they rejoice before you as at the harvest,
 as men make merry when dividing spoils.
For the yoke that burdened them,
 the pole on their shoulder,
And the rod of their taskmaster
 you have smashed, as on the day of Midian.
For every boot that tramped in battle,
 every cloak rolled in blood,
  will be burned as fuel for flames.

For a child is born to us, a son is given us;
 upon his shoulder dominion rests.
They name him Wonder-Counselor, God-Hero,
 Father-Forever, Prince of Peace.
His dominion is vast
 and forever peaceful,
From David's throne, and over his kingdom,
 which he confirms and sustains
By judgment and justice,
 both now and forever.
The zeal of the LORD of hosts will do this!

Isaiah 9:1–16
Mass at Midnight
Roman rite

B UT you, Bethlehem-Ephrathah
Too small to be among the clans of Judah,
From you shall come forth for me
   one who is to be ruler in Israel;
Whose origin is from of old,
   from ancient times.
(Therefore the Lord will give them up, until the time
   when she who is to give birth has borne,
And the rest of his brethren shall return
   to the children of Israel.)
He shall stand firm and shepherd his flock
   by the strength of the Lord, his God;
And they shall remain, for now his greatness
   shall reach to the ends of the earth;
   he shall be peace.

Micah 5:1-3
Reading for
Christmas Day
Byzantine rite

WHAT Adam's disobedience cost,
    let holy scripture say:
ourselves estranged, an Eden lost,
And then a judgment day:
Each day a judgment day.

An Ark of Mercy rode the Flood;
But we, where waters swirled,
Rebuilt, impatient of the good,
Another fallen world:
An unrepentant world.

And now a Child is Adam's heir,
Is Adam's hope, and Lord.
Sing joyful carols everywhere
That Eden is restored:
In Jesus is restored.

Regained is Adam's blessedness;
The angels sheathe their swords.
In joyful carols all confess
The Kingdom is the Lord's:
The glory is the Lord's!

"Adam and Christ"
Fred Pratt Green

CHRISTMAS calls a community back to its origins by remembering Jesus' own beginnings as a human child, a prophet of God's reign, a judgment on the world and its projects. What the parish celebrates during this season is not primarily a birthday, but the beginning of a decisive new phase in the tempestuous history of God's hunger for human companions. The social concerns of the season are thus rooted in Jesus' proclamation of God's reign: the renunciation of patterns that oppress others (holding, climbing, commanding) and the formation of a new human community that voluntarily embraces those renunciations. It is an *adult* Christ that the community encounters during the Advent and Christmas cycles of Sundays and feasts: a Risen Lord who invites sinful people to become church. Christmas does not ask us to pretend we were back in Bethlehem, kneeling before a crib; it asks us to recognize that the wood of the crib became the wood of the cross.

Nathan Mitchell

THE grace of God has appeared, offering salvation to all men. It trains us to reject godless ways and worldly desires, and live temperately, justly, and devoutly in this age as we await our blessed hope, the appearing of the glory of the great God and of our Savior Christ Jesus. It was he who sacrificed himself for us, to redeem us from all unrighteousness and to cleanse for himself a people of his own, eager to do what is right.

Titus 2:11–14
Mass at Midnight
Roman rite

THE blessed Son of God only
In a crib full poor did lie;
With our poor flesh and our poor blood
Was clothed that everlasting good.
Kyrieleison.

The Lord Christ Jesu, God's Son dear,
Was a guest and a stranger here;
Us for to bring from misery,
That we might live eternally.
Kyrieleison.

And this did he for us freely,
For to declare his great mercy
All Christendom be merry therefore,
And give him thanks for evermore.

Miles Coverdale,
after Martin Luther   *Kyrieleison.*

YOU are Holy,
  you who wished to be born in the midst of our sins
the better to pardon us,
        we beg you:
    Lord, have mercy.

  You are Strong,
you who wished to be born weak as a child in order to
give us strength,
        we beg you:
    Christ have mercy.

  You are Immortal,
you who have to put on a body to die
in order to give us immortality,
        we beg you:
    Lord, have mercy.

Holy God, strong God, immortal God,
give the peace of heaven to our earth,
and open the door of your mercy
to the beggars of your love.   Lucien Deiss

THE Word is born this very night:
Hail, Mary, full of grace!
A hanging lantern sheds its light
On Joseph's anxious face.

The Word must come in human form,
In God's redemptive plan.
A Babe takes every heart by storm,
But who will heed the Man?

The Word is born this very night,
And humble is the place;
The world is dark, but hope is bright,
And sinners look for grace.

The Word has come to end the war
Which Adam first began.
O bless the Babe who sleeps on straw.
And listen to the Man!

"The Word
Became Flesh"
Fred Pratt Green

I mean the central Christian fact that God became human.
Without this fact the Catholic enterprise would not make
sense. I say this because it is only the assurance that we know
God fully, clearly, and only, in the human fact of Jesus of Nazareth which makes it impossible to reject any aspect of creation
as irrelevant to the Kingdom of God. Many great spiritual ways
have led towards the experience of God, and clearly they are
true ways, they do lead to that ultimate reality. They often assert

that material reality is full of signs of God, is the vast array of gifts of his providing, is a manifestation of his Being. But only the revelation of God in Christ asserts the being of God fully and accurately present in one unique human person, who is not simply a manifestation of God, but is God.

So the human person is at the heart of an enormously complex, subtle, and varied pattern of interrelated and inter-dependent being, and beings. It follows that if indeed we can say that, in looking at Jesus of Nazareth, we are seeing the reality of God, then we are saying that all material as well as spiritual reality is capable, at a certain point, of being God. It is, of course, the "certain point" that matters. This is not pantheism but incarnation, the entering into material reality, at a given time and place, of the divine reality which always underlies it. This is the stumbling block for many. They can accept the idea of divine immanence, God present in some sense in all things, but not the scandalous particularity of incarnation, which sees not only material reality in general but history — sequence, development, human circumstance and human response — as divinely significant. So God himself enters into a new relationship with matter at a certain point in time, on a certain spot, and as the outcome of an historical and cultural "process," which is not an imposed plan but the decisions and arrangements (for good or ill) of particular people belonging to a particular nation which had particular experiences, both political and religious.

Rosemary Haughton
The Catholic Thing

I N those days Caesar Augustus published a decree ordering a census of the whole world. This first census took place while Quirinius was governor of Syria. Everyone went to register, each to his own town. And so Joseph went from the town of Nazareth in Galilee to Judea, to David's town of Bethlehem—because he was of the house and lineage of David—to register with Mary, his espoused wife, who was with child.

While they were there the days of her confinement were completed. She gave birth to her first-born son and wrapped him in swaddling clothes and laid him in a manger, because there was no room for them in the place where travelers lodged.

There were shepherds in the locality, living in the fields and keeping night watch by turns over their flock. The angel of the Lord appeared to them, as the glory of the Lord shone around them, and they were very much afraid. The angel said to them: "You have nothing to fear! I come to proclaim good news to you—tidings of great joy to be shared by the whole people. This day in David's city a savior has been born to you, the Messiah and Lord. Let this be a sign to you: in a manger you will find an infant wrapped in swaddling clothes." Suddenly, there was with the angel a multitude of the heavenly host, praising God and saying,

"Glory to God in high heaven,

Luke 2:1–14
Mass at Midnight
Roman rite
peace on earth to those on whom his
favor rests."

WIDE, wide in the rose's side
  Sleeps a child without sin,
And any man who loves in this world
Stands here on guard over him.

"Wide, Wide in
the Rose's Side"
Kenneth Patchen

THOU wast born in secret, in a cave,
  But heaven hath told all of thee,
Choosing for its voice a star,
Which hath guided the wise men to worship thee.

Vespers
Orthodox liturgy

I wish you could see your eyes sometimes.
An inner stirring, always a surprise, ever a
Miracle as any growing is,
Brightens the softness brown.
Taking my hand, we touch ripe skin, blanketing
Life fresh and strong.
A man of silences, the movement fills me—carpenter's
Callouses rest upon a smooth heat. My own center
Jumps, a welling up, blinking tears.
A later Daniel, too a prophet, tells the birth of
A Child as "reason enough to trim the lamps of the
Universe, to grace seasons in a wedding garment,
To wreathe in smiles our stiff jointed discontent."
Glory to God, watching you sleep.

"Joseph's Song"
Dennis Kennedy

GOD and father of Jesus,
you have sent your Son to be our savior:
    our light in the midst of darkness,
    our hope in the face of threats,
    our peace amid turmoil.

In this word and sacrament
    we have seen him
    and know that your promises are true.

Send us forth from this assembly
    to live in hope and peace,
    until we gather again at his table.

This we ask in the name of Jesus the Lord.

Mass at Midnight
Contemporary

O Lord, our God, thou didst desire to dwell not only in heaven but also with us on earth, to be not only exalted and great, but like us lowly and small, not only to rule, but to serve us, not only to be God for eternity, but to be born, to live, and to die for us.

In thy dear Son, our Savior Jesus Christ, Thou hast given us no less than thine own self so that we might belong wholly to thee. This concerns us all, although no one of us has earned it. What remains then for us but to be amazed, to rejoice, to be thankful, to hold fast to that which thou hast done for us?

We beseech thee, grant that this may become reality among us and in all at this hour. Grant that in honorable, open, and willing prayer and in song, speaking, and hearing we may become a true Christmas congregation, and in great hunger may experience the true communion of the Lord's Supper. Amen.   Karl Barth

H AND by hand must we take each other
and be blissful and happy;
for man has renounced the devil of hell
and God's son is made our spouse.

A child is born among men,
and in that child was no blemish:
that child is God, that child is man,
and in that child our life began.

Hand by hand must we take each other
and be blissful and happy;
for man has renounced the devil of hell
And God's son is made our spouse.

Medieval English verse

B REAK forth, O beauteous heav'nly light,
And usher in the morning;
Ye shepherds, shrink not with affright,
But hear the angel's warning.
This child, this little helpless boy,
Shall be our confidence and joy,
The powers of hell o'er-throwing,
At last our peace bestowing.

Johann Rist
Seventeenth century

A T Bethlehem born,
at Nazareth brought up,
he lived in Galilee.
A sign in the sky; we saw it ourselves.
How the star shone! The shepherds that night
in the fields fell to their knees in amazement and said:
Glory to the Father, alleluia.
Glory to the Son and Holy Spirit.
Alleluia, alleluia, alleluia!

Fourth century

W HEN the kindness and love of God our savior
appeared, he saved us, not because of any righteous
deeds we had done, but because of his mercy. He saved us
through the baptism of new birth and renewal by the Holy
Spirit. This Spirit he lavished on us through Jesus Christ our
Savior, that we might be justified by his grace and become
heirs, in hope, of eternal life.

Titus 3:4–7
Mass at Dawn
Roman rite

I wonder as I wander, out under the sky,
How Jesus the savior did come for to die
For poor or'n'ry people like you and like I.
I wonder as I wander out under the sky.

When Mary bore Jesus, 'twas in a cow's stall,
With wise men and an'mals and shepherds and all.
But high from the heavens a star's light did fall,
and the promise of ages it then did recall.

If Jesus had wanted for any small thing,
A star in the sky or a bird on the wing,
Or all of God's angels in heav'n for to sing,
He could sure have had it, 'cause he was the King.

I wonder as I wander, out under the sky,
How Jesus the savior did come for to die
For poor or'n'ry people like you and like I,
I wonder as I wander out under the sky.

Traditional
North Carolina carol

WHEN the angels had returned to heaven, the shepherds said to one another: "Let us go over to Bethlehem and see this event which the Lord has made known to us." They went in haste and found Mary and Joseph, and the baby lying in the manger; once they saw, they understood what had been told them concerning this child. All who heard of it were astonished at the report given them by the shepherds.

Mary treasured all these things and reflected on them in her heart. The shepherds returned, glorifying and praising God for all they had heard and seen, in accord with what had been told them.

Luke 2:15-20
Mass at Dawn
Roman rite

M ARY speaks for all those who have been lowly, on the outside, at the bottom, colonized, suppressed, and totally outside of the halls of the princes and power wielders. If she has been favored and blessed, if she is a sign of the ultimate and greatest power, then the lowly who follow her can believe themselves favored and backed up by the universe. They may make their demands and unite against the princes who oppress them. If the hidden is real, if it is true that spiritual power is greater than the power of guns and bombs, then the lowly and the oppressed have hope. If the Almighty sides with justice, hopes can be fulfilled and all can win equality.

It is no accident that almost always the cult of Mary has been a cult of the people. Everywhere "folk Catholicism" has maintained a devotion to Mary in the face of opposition and disparagement from theologians and leaders of church and state. True the major central doctrines of Christianity were frequently obscured by crude superstitions and by importation of pagan myths and rites into the cult of Mary. But as at the beginning of the devotion of Mary and in the first developments of understanding of her, perhaps it has been something more subtle which has fired this devotion. Perhaps it has been the realization in Marian cultic practice of the importance of the lowly and humble and outcast and oppressed who will triumph in the end. If Mary, the young unmarried pregnant girl, can believe in the incredible happening that she is a part of, if she can trust herself and believe in her role in the great story, then the most ordinary people can believe in their parts in the drama. Her exaltation is their exaltation. She carries the banner for all those powerless ones whom the princes have ignored as they go to and fro on the earth making policy, making war, making fortunes, and bringing destruction everywhere. Mary is the champion for all the obscure, peaceful ones who live in the corners of the world, who work, who help each other, who bear children and hope to see them live and prosper—those who do not aspire to the thrones and the vanities of princes.

The poor may have seen a defender of their cause in the woman and mother. She is beloved in an infinite variety of feminine forms, from young virgin to older mother. By exalting Mary as queen of mercy, queen of peace, a mother most gracious, a mother most wise, in all of the traditional devotions, there has been a hope that the feminine qualities which have been demeaned for so long in our society could have their day and could be influential in ordinary life. The high, cool exercise of power and judgment was never seen as part of Mary's role. She never rejected the poor and the lowly or those who tried and met failure time after time. While Christ's mercy and tenderness and feminine qualities were often obscured by the male princes and powers who fought in his name and killed in his honor and taxed for his representatives, still Mary as mother could guard that aspect of the Christian message which her son's followers hid so successfully.

Sidney Callahan
The Magnificat

O my child, child of sweetness,
  How is it that I hold thee, Almighty?
And how that I feed thee,
Who givest bread to all?
How is it that I swaddle thee,
Who with the clouds encompasseth the whole earth?   Orthodox liturgy

L o, how a rose e'er blooming
  From tender stem hath sprung
Of Jesse's lineage coming
as prophets long have sung,
It came a flow'ret bright
Amid the cold of winter
When half spent was the night.

Isaiah 'twas foretold it
The rose I have in mind.
With Mary we behold it
The Virgin mother kind.
To show God's love aright
She bore to us a savior
When half spent was the night.   Sixteenth century

T WAS in the moon of wintertime
When all the birds had fled,
That God, the Lord of all the earth,
Sent angel choirs instead.
Before their light the stars grew dim,
And wond'ring hunters heard the hymn:
Jesus your king is born! Jesus is born!
Glory be to God on high!

The earliest moon of wintertime
Is not so round and fair
As was the ring of glory
Around the infant there.
And when the shepherds then drew near
The angel voices rang out clear:
Jesus your king is born! Jesus is born!
Glory be to God on high!

O children of the forest free,
The angels' song is true.
The holy child of earth and heav'n
Is born today for you.
Come, kneel before the radiant boy,
Who brings you beauty, peace, and joy.
Jesus your king is born! Jesus is born!
Glory be to God on high!

Jean de Brebeuf
Seventeenth century

D AUGHTER of Zion, exult; shout aloud, daughter of Jerusalem! Your King is coming, the Holy One, the savior of
the world.

Mass at Dawn
Roman rite

WHOM have you seen, O shepherds?
Speak, tell us, who has appeared on earth?
"A child we saw, and choirs of angels praising the Lord!"
Speak, what did you see? and proclaim the birth of
 Christ!

Matins
Divine Office
Roman rite

FROM east to west, from shore to shore,
Let ev'ry heart awake and sing
The holy child whom Mary bore,
The Christ, the everlasting king.

Behold, the world's creator wears
The form and fashion of a slave;
Our very flesh our maker shares,
His fallen creatures, all, to save.

For this how wondrously he wrought!
A maiden, in her lowly place
Became, in ways beyond all thought,
The chosen vessel of his grace.

And while the angels in the sky
Sang praise above the silent field,
To shepherds poor the Lord most high,
The one great shepherd, was revealed.

All glory for this blessed morn
To God the Father ever be;
All praise to you, O Virgin-born,
And Holy Ghost, eternally. Amen

Christmas lauds hymn
Roman rite

Augustine
Fifth century

LET us celebrate this day not because of the visible sun, but because of him who made this day.

THIS day true peace has come down to us from heaven,
this day the heavens drip honey upon the entire world.
This day brought the dawn of new redemption,
of the deliverance announced of old, of eternal happiness.

Matins
Divine Office
Roman rite

THE whole church rejoices today, Almighty Father, for thine only Son, whom the prophets foretold, came into this world as dew upon the grass and made joy to spring up abundantly. Therefore the earth also sings her delight, for, watered by the rain from heaven, she offers wonderful gifts to her redeemer.

Christmas collect
An old Ravenna rite

YOUR nativity, O Christ our God, has shed the light of knowledge upon the world. Through it, those who had been star-worshipers learned through a star to worship you, O Sun of Justice, and to recognize in you the one who rises and who comes from on high. O Lord, glory to you!

Orthodox liturgy
Feast of the Nativity

LET us dance with delight in the Lord and let our hearts be filled with rejoicing, for eternal salvation has appeared on the earth, alleluia.

Liturgy of the Hours
Roman rite

WONDERFUL the dignity you bestowed, O God, on human nature when you created it; more wonderful still its condition when you recreated it. Grant, we pray, that as Jesus Christ, your Son, stooped to share our human nature, so we may share the lot of his divine nature. Through that same Jesus Christ, your Son, our Lord, who with you and the Holy Spirit has shared one life and kingly power, one godhead, from all eternity.

Leonine Sacramentary
Early sixth century

Traditional collect
for the Nativity
of our Lord
*The Book of
Common Prayer*

O God, who makest us glad with the yearly remembrance of the birth of thy only Son Jesus Christ: Grant that as we joyfully receive him for our Redeemer, so we may with sure confidence behold him when he shall come to be our Judge.

Leonine Sacramentary
Early sixth century

GRANT, we pray you, merciful God, God of unlimited power, Father from all eternity—that the feast of our Lord's nativity—Jesus Christ's—to which these rites are a prelude, may be something new to us. May it not pass away but continue for ever, so that the wonder of it will always be new.

How beautiful upon the mountains
are the feet of him who brings glad tidings,
Announcing peace, bearing good news,
    announcing salvation, and saying to Zion,
    "Your God is King!"

Hark! Your watchmen raise a cry,
    together they shout for joy,
For they see directly, before their eyes,
    the Lord restoring Zion.
Break out together in song,
    O ruins of Jerusalem!
For the Lord comforts his people,
    he redeems Jerusalem.
The Lord has bared his holy arm
    in the sight of all the nations;
All the ends of the earth will behold
    the salvation of our God.

Isaiah 52:7–10
Mass during the Day
Roman rite

The Father, who at the beginning created all things, has
sent his Son to restore them and bring them back to their
former state. In fact, he renewed the whole world which
Adam, stripped of his youthfulness after his sin, had caused
to fall into ruin. The creator of all things became the restorer.
He gave them back their former beauty.

Ephraem
Second century

CHRISTMAS 1970

Tomorrow shall be my dancing day.
I would my true love did so chance
To see the legend of my play
To call my true love to my dance.
  Sing, O my love, O my love, my love, my love.
  This have I done for my true love.

In a manger laid and wrapped I was,
So very poor, this was my chance,
Betwixt an ox and a silly poor ass,
To call my true love to my dance.

Christmas is an ancient feast of frivolity (the Puritans forbade it!) and this English carol seems to have caught that spirit, anticipating the current "theology of play." If we wish you a playful, dancing, merry Christmas our intention is not the hope that you will find some rough mockery of the ecstasy, the pattern, the joy and the grace of the Ancient Dance in the frenzied days, the harried attempts to make sense of our lives, the half-guilty celebrations, the stilted human relationships which mark our fasts and fill our days.

It is rather the hope that you may perceive the legend of God's play: "this have I done for my true love"—and that the festival of this prodigality will strengthen and deepen the elements of the Dance in your life: love and forgiveness and mystery and harmony and grace and attention and wonder and jubilation and praise and bodiliness and freedom and a *pas de deux* spontaneously discovered for a few moments or labored out over faithful years.

In this year of the plod and march of technology and war, of
our own plod and march we wish you the Dance of the Word
of God. Now he shares our poverty and there is a chance.

> I know nothing, except what everyone
> knows—if there when Grace dances,
> I should dance.
>
> W. H. Auden

Gordon Lathrop
Christmas greeting

SING to the LORD a new song;
sing to the LORD, all you lands.
Sing to the LORD; bless his name;
  announce his salvation, day after day.
Tell his glory among the nations;
  among all peoples, his wondrous deeds.

For great is the LORD and highly to be praised;
  awesome is he, beyond all gods.
For all the gods of the nations are things of nought,
  but the LORD made the heavens.
Splendor and majesty go before him;
  Praise and grandeur are in his sanctuary.

Give to the LORD, you families of nations,
  give to the LORD glory and praise;
  give to the LORD the glory due his name!
Bring gifts, and enter his courts;
  worship the LORD in holy attire.
Tremble before him, all the earth;
  say among the nations: The LORD is king.
He has made the world firm, not to be moved;
  he governs the peoples with equity.

Let the heavens be glad and the earth rejoice;
   let the sea and what fills it resound;
   let the plains be joyful and all that is in them!
Then shall all the trees of the forest exult
   before the LORD, for he comes;
   for he comes to rule the earth.
He shall rule the world with justice
Psalm 96   and the peoples with his constancy.

WISDOM is the refulgence of eternal light,
   the spotless mirror of the power of God,
the image of his goodness,
And she, who is one, can do all things,
   and renews everything while herself perduring;
And passing into holy souls from age to age,
   she produces friends of God and prophets.

Wisdom 7:26-27
Liturgy of the Hours
Thursday from
January 2 to Epiphany
Roman rite

I N times past, God spoke in fragmentary and varied ways to
our fathers through the prophets; in this, the final age, he
has spoken to us through his Son, whom he has made heir of
all things and through whom he first created the universe.
This Son is the reflection of the Father's glory, the exact
representation of the Father's being, and he sustains all
things by his powerful word. When the Son had cleansed us
from our sins, he took his seat at the right hand of the Majesty
in heaven, as far superior to the angels as the name he has
inherited is superior to theirs.

To which of the angels did God ever say,
    "You are my son; today I have begotten you"?
Or again,
    "I will be his father, and he shall be my son"?
And again when he leads his first-born into the world, he
        says,
    "Let all the angels of God worship him."

Hebrews 1:1–6
Mass during the Day
Roman rite

L ET all the earth bow to you and sing to you,
Let all sing your name Most High.

Orthodox Liturgy

O Savior of our fallen race,
O brightness of the Father's face,
O Son who shared the Father's might
Before the world knew day or night,

O Jesus, very Light of light,
Our constant star in sin's deep night:
Now hear the prayers your people pray
Throughout the world this holy day.

Remember, Lord of life and grace,
How once, to save our fallen race,
You put our human vesture on
And came to us as Mary's son.

Today, as year by year its light
Bathes all the world in radiance bright,
One precious truth outshines the sun:
Salvation comes from you alone.

For from the Father's throne you came,
His banished children to reclaim;
And earth and sea and sky revere
The love of him who sent you here.

And we are jubilant today,
For you have washed our guilt away.
Oh, hear the glad new song we sing
On this, the birthday of our king!

O Christ, redeemer virgin-born,
Let songs of praise your name adorn,
Whom with the Father we adore
And Holy Spirit evermore. Amen.

Vespers hymn
Sixth century
Divine Office
Roman rite

THE radiance of the Father's splendor, the Father's visible image, Jesus Christ our God, peerless among counselors, prince of peace, father of the world to come, the model after which Adam was formed, for our sakes became like a slave: in the womb of Mary the virgin, without assistance from any man, he took flesh. For our sakes he was wrapped in swaddling-clothes, laid in a manger and praised by the angelic powers.

"Glory to God in high heaven," they sang; "peace and good will to men."

Enable us, Lord, to reach the end of this luminous feast in peace, forsaking all idle words, acting virtuously, shunning our passions and raising ourselves above the things of this world. . . .

May we celebrate your glorious birth, and the Father who sent you to redeem us, and your Spirit, the giver of life, now and for ever, age after age. Amen.   Syriac

I N the beginning was the Word;
the Word was in God's presence,
  and the Word was God.
  He was present to God in the beginning.
  Through him all things came into being,
  and apart from him nothing came to be.
  Whatever came to be in him, found life,
  life for the light of men.
  The light shines on in darkness,
  a darkness that did not overcome it.
The real light which gives light to every man was coming
into the world.
  He was in the world
  and through him the world was made,
  yet the world did not know who he was.
  To his own he came,
  yet his own did not accept him.
  Any who did accept him
  he empowered to become children of God.
These are they who believe in his name—who were
begotten not by blood, nor by carnal desire, nor by man's
willing it, but by God.
  The Word became flesh
  and made his dwelling among us,
  and we have seen his glory:
  the glory of an only Son coming from the Father,
  filled with enduring love.

John 1:1-5, 9-14
Mass during the Day
Roman rite

GIDEON'S threshing floor is
drenched with dew from heaven,
and the flame burning in the bush
shines without heat.
The earthen vessel
brings forth the seed from a seed,
the golden light!
The good grain comes out of the chaff,
the olive from the olive trees,
and the rock flows with water.

Medieval
Processional song

A marvelous change was wrought in our nature at its
restoration. This truth flashed on the world when from
the old stock the new humanity was born, from mortality
came immortality, from human nature the remedy was drawn
for human nature's healing, from a race of sinners sprang a
child who was innocent of sin. When your Word took to himself this frail nature of ours, it was honored with the gift of
eternity and we ourselves, sharing its wonderful destiny, were
made eternal also.

The Leonine
Sacramentary
Sixth century

Irenaeus
Third century

BECAUSE of his boundless love, Jesus became what we are that he might make us to be what he is.

THY epiphany, O Lord, made the earth leap for joy. . . . The choir of shepherds on earth glorified thy all-saving advent.

Today, the Word who sits on the throne of glory with the Father became flesh, born of the holy Virgin, giving the universe the grace of adoption.

Ephraem
Fourth century

C HRIST is born. He is born *to us*. And, He is born *today*. For Christmas is not merely a day like every other day. It is a day made holy and special by a sacred mystery. It is not merely another day in the weary round of time. Today, eternity enters into time, and time, sanctified, is caught up into eternity. Today, Christ, the eternal Word of the Father, who was in the beginning with the Father, in whom all things were made, by whom all things consist, enters into the world which he created in order to reclaim souls who had forgotten their identity. Therefore, the church exults, as the angels come down to announce not merely an old thing which happened long ago, but a new thing which happens today. For today, God the Father makes all things new, in his divine Son, our redeemer, according to his words: *ecce nova facio omnia*.

Therefore, the church on earth joins with the church in heaven to sing one same song, the new song, the *canticum novum* which the prophet commanded all to sing after the world should have been redeemed by the Christ, whose ancestor he knew, by revelation, that he should be. When David cried out: "Sing to the Lord a new song" he was the first precentor to intone the songs the church would sing on this day in her liturgy, as she announces to the whole world salvation and joy. For as St. Leo says: "Today there has shone upon us a day of new redemption, a day restoring that which was long lost, a day of bliss unending."

Thomas Merton

CHRIST is born: give him glory!
Christ has come down from heaven: receive him!
Christ is now on earth: exalt him!
O you earth, sing to the Lord!
O you nations, praise him in joy, for he has been
   glorified!

Christmas canon
Orthodox liturgy

DEARLY beloved, today our Savior is born; let us rejoice. Sadness should have no place on the birthday of life. The fear of death has been swallowed up; life brings us joy with the promise of eternal happiness.

No one is shut out from this joy; all share the same reason for rejoicing. Our Lord, victor over sin and death, finding no one free from sin, came to free us all. Let the saint rejoice—seeing the palm of victory at hand. Let the sinner be glad—receiving the offer of forgiveness. Let the pagan take courage—being summoned to life. . . .

Christian, remember your dignity, and now that you share in God's own nature, do not return by sin to your former base condition. Bear in mind who is your head and of whose body you are a member. Do not forget that you have been rescued from the power of darkness and brought into the light of God's kingdom.

Leo the Great
Fifth century
Office of Readings
Roman rite

COME, then, let us observe the feast. Come, and we shall commemorate the solemn festival. It is a strange manner of celebrating a festival; but truly wondrous is the whole chronicle of the nativity. For this day the ancient slavery is ended, the devil confounded, the demons take to flight, the power of death is broken, paradise is unlocked, the curse is taken away, sin is removed from us, error driven out, truth has been brought back, the speech of kindliness diffused, and spreads on every side, a heavenly way of life has been implanted on the earth, angels communicate with men without fear, and men now hold speech with angels.

Why is this? Because God is now on earth, and man in heaven; on every side all things commingle. He has come on earth, while being whole in heaven; and while complete in heaven, he is without diminution on earth. Though he was God, he became man; not denying himself to be God. Though being the impassable Word, he became flesh; that he might dwell amongst us. He became flesh. He did not become God. He was God. Wherefore he became flesh, so that he whom heaven did not contain, a manger would this day receive. He was placed in a manger, so that he, by whom all things are nourished, may receive an infant's food from his virgin mother. So, the father of all ages, as an infant at the breast, nestles in the virginal arms, that the magi may more easily see him.

John Chrysostom
Fifth century

TODAY the darkness begins to grow shorter and the light to lengthen, as the hours of night become fewer. Nor is it an accident . . . that this change occurs on the solemn day when divine life is manifested. . . . Rather, to those who are attentive, nature manifests through visible things a hidden reality. . . . I seem to hear her saying: "Realize . . . as you observe these phenomena, that the invisible is being manifested to you through the visible. You see, do you not, that night has reached its greatest length, and since it can advance no farther, comes to a halt and withdraws? . . . Do you see that the beams of light are more intense and the sun higher than it has been? Realize that the true light is now here and, through the rays of the gospel, is illumining the whole earth.

Gregory of Nyssa
Fourth century

JESUS, Son of the living God, splendor of the Father, light
eternal, king of glory, sun of justice, born of the virgin
Mary:
Glory to you, O Lord!
Jesus, wonderful counselor, strong Lord, eternal God,
prince of peace:
Glory to you, O Lord!
Jesus, most powerful, patient, obedient, gentle and
humble of heart, loving all who are pure in heart:
Glory to you, O Lord!
Jesus, God of peace, source of life, pattern of
holiness, friend of all, our God and our refuge:
Glory to you, O Lord!
Jesus, brother of the poor, treasure of the faithful,
good shepherd, true light, inexhaustible wisdom,
boundless love, our way and our life:
Glory to you, O Lord!
Jesus, joy of the angels, king of the patriarchs,
master of the apostles, teacher of the evangelists,
strength of the martyrs, light of every witness to
the truth, crown of all the saints:
Glory to you, O Lord!

Praise God:
Common Prayer
at Taize

O Lord, our God! Thou art great, holy, and exalted above us and all humankind. And now thou art great in that thou wast unwilling to forget us, to leave alone, or, in spite of all that speaks against us, to reject us. Now hast thou given us in thy dear Son Jesus Christ, our Lord, nothing less than thine own self and all that is thine. We thank thee that we are privileged to be thy guests at the table of thy grace, as long as we live, and for eternity.

We bring now before thee all that troubles us: our failings, errors, and exaggerations, our tribulations, our sorrows, and also our rebelliousness and bitterness—our whole heart, our whole life, which thou knowest better than we ourselves. We place it all in the faithful hands which thou hast stretched out to us in our savior. Take us as we are; raise up those who are poor.

And so let thy friendship illumine our families and all those who are captive or suffer need or are sick or near death. Give those who judge the spirit of righteousness and those who bear rule in the world a measure of thy wisdom that they may think of peace on earth. Give clarity and courage to those who at home or as missionaries abroad proclaim thy word!

And now we bring all our petitions together as we call on thee
Karl Barth   as our Savior has allowed and bidden us: Our Father . . .

READINGS FOR THE FEAST OF THE NATIVITY
IN THE ORTHODOX LITURGY

Genesis 1:1–13
Verses from Numbers 24
Micah 4:6–7
Micah 5:1–3
Isaiah 11:1–10
Baruch 3:35 and 4:4
Daniel 2:31–36, 44–45
Isaiah 8:3–6
Isaiah 7:10–16; 8:1–4 and 9:8–10
Hebrews 1:1–12
Luke 2:1–20

FATHER, all-powerful and ever-living God,
we do well always and everywhere to give you thanks
through Jesus Christ our Lord.

In the wonder of the incarnation
your eternal Word has brought to the eyes of faith
a new and radiant vision of your glory.
In him we see our God made visible
and so are caught up in love of the God we cannot see.

Preface of Christmas I
Roman rite

FATHER, all-powerful and ever-living God,
we do well always and everywhere to give you
thanks
through Jesus Christ our Lord.

Today you fill our hearts with joy
as we recognize in Christ the revelation of your love.
No eye can see his glory as our God,
yet now he is seen as one like us.

Christ is your Son before all ages,
yet now he is born in time.
He has come to lift up all things to himself,
to restore unity to creation,
and to lead mankind from exile into your heavenly
kingdom.

Preface of Christmas II
Roman rite

HODIE Christus natus est:
Hodie salvator apparuit:
Hodie in terra canunt angeli,
laetantur archangeli:
Hodie exultant justi, dicentes:
Gloria in excelsis Deo: Alleluia.

This day Christ is born;
This day the savior has appeared;
This day angels are singing on earth,
archangels are rejoicing;
This day the just are glad and say:
Glory to God in the highest, alleluia!

Magnificat antiphon
Divine Office
Roman rite

WE can keep all our modern, beloved Christmas trappings, as long as we see through them and as long as we know that there is a reality and a future behind those things of the past. When we celebrate Midnight Mass in Bethlehem "at the crib," as the missal says; when we go as good pilgrims to the Mass "at dawn" in the Church of the *Anastasis* (Resurrection); and when we see the full glory of the divine child in the third Mass, we have already made a seven-league step from the crib idyll toward the full meaning of the parousia. . . . Certainly our crib and customs have their place, and nobody will take them away; but their place is the foreground, the emotional, historical, meditative side of our religious being. Still while the world moves on in powerful strides and groans for redemption, let us not forget that it was not the babe who redeemed it, but the babe grown man, crucified, resurrected, and sitting at the right hand of the Father, whence he will come to *judge* the living and the dead.   H. A. Reinhold

JUST as it is the crucified who is "Messiah," so it is the crucified who is Sun and Light-Tree and the end of darkness and the world's health. That is evident in the liturgy by all the light themes being sung at *mass*, the Christ-mass, at the meal which proclaims Christ's death until he comes. . . . It is further evident in the themes of the littleness and hiddenness and humility of the birth—present in hymnody and readings—themselves sub-themes of the cross, or in the *cross* references of the readings ("a sword will pierce through your own soul also"), or, most especially in the feasts which have very anciently accompanied the day of Christmas (the feasts of the *comites Christi*, Durandus called them in the thirteenth century, the "companions of Christ"). *This* sun is hated by the rulers of the world and his cross is foreshadowed in the sufferings of the Innocents and in all unjust sufferings. *This* Sun ("I see the heavens opened and the Son of man standing at the right hand of God.") [cf. Roman liturgy readings for St. Stephen] invites to witness and to a martyrdom parallel to his own.

So it is that our Christmas comes to have the *admirabile commercium*, "the wonderful exchange," as its central theme—our wretchedness for his blessedness, as Luther would say. Or so it is "only in these our Christian mysteries that we can rejoice and mourn at once for the same reason" (T. S. Eliot in *Murder in the Cathedral*).

Gordon Lathrop

EVEN the oldest liturgical calendars already have a series of saints' feasts directly following on Christmas. The Middle Ages saw these saints as a cortege of honor accompanying the Christ-child, and gave them the name *Comites Christi* ("Companions of Christ"). In the Roman liturgy these companions are Stephen the first martyr on December 26, John the Apostle and Evangelist on December 27, and the children whom Herod slew in Bethlehem on December 28. . . . The feast of St. Stephen dates from the fourth century in the East, in the West it is known from the beginning of the fifth. . . .

The feast of John the Apostle and Evangelist also goes back to the fourth century in the East; it was originally accompanied by a commemoration of his brother, James the Greater. . . . From the early Middle Ages down to our own day the custom of blessing and distributing "St. John's wine" has been observed. It is connected with the pagan custom (among Greeks, Romans, Germans) of partaking of a drink in honor of a god. Once Christianity had been introduced, the custom became one of drinking to the honor of certain saints. . . . The drink in loving memory of John acquired special significance and lasting popularity once an official blessing of St. John's wine had been instituted. The blessing in turn was certainly connected with the legend of [St. John's] drinking of the poisoned wine.

The feast of the Holy Innocents on December 28 seems to be a Western creation. The first mention of it occurs in the calendar of the North African city of Carthage for 505. . . . The connection with the events of Christmas certainly influenced the choice of a date for the feast.   Adolf Adam

JESUS said to his apostles: "Be on your guard with respect to others. They will hale you into court, they will flog you in their synagogues. You will be brought to trial before rulers and kings, to give witness before them and before the Gentiles on my account. When they hand you over, do not worry about what you will say or how you will say it. When the hour comes, you will be given what you are to say. You yourselves will not be the speakers; the Spirit of your Father will be speaking in you.

"Brother will hand over brother to death, and the father his child; children will turn against parents and have them put to death. You will be hated by all on account of me. But whoever holds out till the end will escape death."

Matthew 10:17–22
Feast of Stephen
Roman rite

GOD is light;
in him there is no darkness.
If we walk in light,
as he is in the light,
we have fellowship with one another,
and the blood of his Son Jesus cleanses us from all sin.

1 John 1:5–5b, 7
Feast of Stephen
Evening Prayer
Roman rite

YESTERDAY we celebrated the birth in time of our eternal King. Today we celebrate the triumphant suffering of his soldier. Yesterday our king, clothed in his robe of flesh, left his place in the virgin's womb and graciously visited the world. Today his soldier leaves the tabernacle of his body and goes triumphantly to heaven.

Our king, despite his exalted majesty, came in humility for our sake; yet he did not come empty-handed. He gave of his bounty, yet without any loss to himself. In a marvelous way he changed into wealth the poverty of his faithful followers while remaining in full possession of his own inexhaustible riches.

And so the love that brought Christ from heaven to earth raised Stephen from earth to heaven; shown first in the king, it later shone forth in his soldier. His love of God kept him from yielding to the ferocious mob; his love for his neighbor made him pray for those who were stoning him. Love inspired him to reprove those who erred, to make them amend; love led him to pray for those who stoned him, to save them from punishment.

Love, indeed, is the source of all good things; it is an impregnable defense, and the way that leads to heaven. He who walks in love can neither go astray nor be afraid: love guides him, protects him, and brings him to his journey's end.

Christ made love the stairway that would enable all Christians to climb to heaven. Hold fast to it, therefore, in all sincerity, give one another practical proof of it, and by your progress in it, make your ascent together.

Fulgentius
Sixth century
Feast of Stephen
Office of Readings
Roman rite

THIS is what we proclaim to you:
what was from the beginning,
what we have heard,
what we have seen with our eyes,
what we have looked upon
and our hands have touched—
we speak of the word of life.
(This life became visible;
we have seen and bear witness to it,
and we proclaim to you the eternal life
that was present to the Father
and became visible to us.)
What we have seen and heard
we proclaim in turn to you
so that you may share life with us.
This fellowship of ours is with the Father
and with his Son, Jesus Christ.
Indeed, our purpose in writing you this
is that our joy may be complete.

1 John 1:1–4
Feast of John
Roman rite

ALMIGHTY Father,
St. John proclaimed that your Word became flesh for our
salvation. Through this eucharist may your Son always live in
us, for he is Lord for ever and ever.

Prayer after
communion
Feast of John
Roman rite

C ONSIDER what is said to you: Love God. If you say to me: Show me whom I am to love, what shall I say if not what Saint John says: *No one has ever seen God!* But in case you should think that you are completely cut off from the sight of God, he says: *God is love, and he who remains in love remains in God.* Love your neighbor, then, and see within yourself the power by which you love your neighbor; there you will see God, as far as you are able.

Begin, then, to love your neighbor. *Break your bread to feed the hungry, and bring into your home the homeless poor; if you see someone naked, clothe him, and do not look down on your own flesh and blood.*

What will you gain by doing this? *Your light will then burst forth like the dawn.* Your light is your God; he is your *dawn*, for he will come to you when the night of time is over. He does not rise or set but remains for ever.

In loving and caring for your neighbor you are on a journey. Where are you traveling if not to the Lord God, to him whom we should love with our whole heart, our whole soul, our whole mind? We have not yet reached his presence, but we have our neighbor at our side. Support, then, this companion of your pilgrimage if you want to come into the presence of the one with whom you desire to remain for ever.

Augustine
Fourth century
Office of Readings
Roman rite

Divine Office
Roman rite
A voice is heard in Rama, crying and weeping,
Rachel weeping for her children.

THE echo of those who weep for the young children
Makes a crash like thunder on the earth,
For the hills and ravines and deep valleys of the
mountains cried aloud in answer.
As though imitating the wailing,
They practiced beats of lamentation with one another.
It was necessary to see the earth full of blood,
And the desert and the uninhabited places,
For this lawless and very arrogant man extended
His anger right up to these places.
For he pursued the mothers and when he caught up
with them
He snatched the children from their very arms, like the
fledgling of a sparrow singing a sweet song.
And he slaughtered them, not understanding, the
wicked fellow,
That in spite of doing these things,
His power will soon be destroyed.

Romanos
Sixth century

THE tyrant broods uneasily:
a prince is born who shall be king
and rule the house of Israel
and occupy great David's throne.

Witless, he raves: "We are deposed:
he that shall oust us is at hand.
Go, guard, and draw your skillful sword,
and foul his little nest with blood."

So fell those flowers of martyrdom
when life was at its dawn for them:
to pluck Christ up he dashed them down,
as wild winds dash the new-born roses.

Are these the first blood-offerings
to come before the Christ—a band
of babies playing on the altar-steps
with palms and coronets?

What use this rash enormity?
What profit in this wasteful wrong?   Prudentius
So many deaths, and Christ alone   Fifth century
escapes from Herod's questing hand.   Divine Office
                                         Roman rite

L IKE most other peoples, the Christian people have waited for the solstice. We have waited, and called those waiting days "Advent." We have waited to tell the stories and sing the songs and pray the prayers. We have waited to put into word and melody and procession all that we want to stake our lives on: this place, this earth, this flesh—God's dwelling place.

Before there were theologies for that, there were stories and around the stories there came to be festivity. The stories were not histories or documentaries. They were tales told about a birth by people who had to see everything through the other end of life, the death in which this Jesus triumphed. And so they told of a woman from Galilee called Mary who (as the poet Gerard Manley Hopkins wrote)

> Gave God's infinity
> Dwindled to infancy
> Welcome in womb and breast,
> Birth, milk, and all the rest. . . .

There was this birth. There was the bursting of waters, blood, pushing, cutting cord, fondly wrapping. There was parting at the beginning, as at every beginning. And not only, the stories tell, the blood of birth spilled, but other blood, the world's most innocent blood. It is a true story being told for that, we know, is the way it goes, the way it went, the way it will go: We've all known kings like Herod. It's practically a prerequisite for the job: "Sure, somebody's going to get hurt, a few lives lost, but isn't it worth it?" It comes with the territory.

But then consider how the medieval drama called "The Play of Herod" ends: the escape to Egypt, the hasty retreat of the magi, then the intrusion of the military into the village. The children are murdered and Rachel — the biblical mother — weeps and laments. A comforter is sent by God, but she refuses to be comforted because her children are no more. But this is not the end of the play. Did they somehow invent a happy ending? Nothing of the kind. The ending is not happy, it is a great mystery. For there is a *Te Deum* sung: "We praise you, God, we confess you as Lord." The greatest chant of praise. This is sung by Mary and Joseph, processing through the audience, but they are joined in their song and procession by the animals and the angels, by the shepherds, by the lamenting Rachel and the parents of Bethlehem, and they are joined by the soldiers and their victims and by Herod. Knowing that (Hopkins again)

we are wound

With mercy round and round. . . .

they all, incarnate God and all creation, even death, tyrants and martyrs, all process and all sing praise. And we sing too, and find ourselves in the procession.

Today we can't imagine it. We take our Christmas with lots of sugar. And take it in a day. Though we've been baptized into his death, we have little time for or patience with how that death is told at Christmas, a death that confuses lament and praise forever. And no wonder we are careful to keep Christmas at an arm's length. What is Herod is these times?

O the night of the weeping children!
O the night of the children branded for death!
Sleep may not enter here. . . .
Yesterday Mother still drew
Sleep toward them like a white moon. . . .
Now blows the wind of dying,
Blows the shifts over the hair
That no one will comb again.*

Not about Bethlemen but about Auschwitz. Or maybe about anyplace the world's Herods (include us in) have wandered. From this year's news: how many places, how many innocent?

Where is that mystery in our Christmastime, the mystery that is victorious cross? It is right there in the stories we tell, the carols we sing, the gifts we give and cards we write, the time we take to process through the dozen days from Christmas to Epiphany, the many ways we have to whisper to one another that the days are numbered now for the world's business-as-usual: somehow, some way we are going to join hands and take the procession all over this earth.

Gabe Huck

*Nelly Sachs: *O The Chimneys* (New York: Farrar, Straus and Giroux, 1967), p. 7.

A s yet heaven and earth are not united. The star of Bethlehem is a star shining in a dark night, even today. On the second day the church already lays aside her white festive vestments and clothes herself in the color of blood, and on the fourth day in the purple of mourning. For the crib of the child is surrounded by martyrs. There is Stephen, the first martyr to follow his Lord to death; there are the innocent children, the babes of Bethlehem and Juda, who were cruelly slaughtered by the hands of brutal hangmen. What does this mean? Where is now the rejoicing of the heavenly hosts, the silent bliss of the holy night? Where is the peace on earth? Peace on earth to those of good will. But not all are of good will. For the Son of the eternal Father descended from the glory of heaven, because the mystery of iniquity had shrouded the earth in the darkness of night.

Edith Stein

S WEET little Jesus Boy,
They made you be born in a manger.
Dear little holy child,
And they didn't know who you was.
Didn't know you came to save us, Lord,
To take our sins away.
Our eyes were blind, we could not see.
We didn't know who you was.

Long time ago, you was born,
Born in a manger low,
Sweet little Jesus Boy.
The world treat you mean, Lord.
Treat me mean, too,
But that's how things is down here.
We didn't know 'twas you!

Sweet little Jesus Boy,
Born long time ago,
Dear little holy child,
And we didn't know who you was!

Robert Macgimsy

W E remember today, O God, the slaughter of the holy
innocents of Bethlehem by King Herod. Receive, we
pray, into the arms of your mercy all innocent victims; and
by your great might frustrate the designs of evil tyrants and
establish your rule of justice, love, and peace; through Jesus
Christ our Lord, who lives and reigns with you, in the unity of
the Holy Spirit, one God, for ever and ever. Amen.

Collect for the
Holy Innocents
Episcopal

Evening Prayer
Liturgy of the Hours
Roman rite

O radiant child! You brought healing to human life as you came forth from the womb of Mary, your mother, like the bridegroom from his marriage chamber.

B E merry, be merry,
I pray you every one!

A principal point of charity
It is, merry to be in him
That is but one. Be merry!

For of a maiden a child
Was born to save mankind
That was forlorn. Be merry!

Now Mary for thy Sonnes sake
Save them alle that mirthe make

Medieval English carol   And longest holdy on! Be merry!

BECAUSE you are God's chosen ones, holy and beloved, clothe yourselves with heartfelt mercy, with kindness, humility, meekness, and patience. Bear with one another; forgive whatever grievances you have against one another. Forgive as the Lord has forgiven you. Over all these virtues put on love, which binds the rest together and makes them perfect. Christ's peace must reign in your hearts, since as members of the one body you have been called to that peace. Dedicate yourselves to thankfulness. Let the word of Christ, rich as it is, dwell in you. In wisdom made perfect, instruct and admonish one another. Sing gratefully to God from your hearts in psalms, hymns, and inspired songs. Whatever you do, whether in speech or in action, do it in the name of the Lord Jesus. Give thanks to God the Father through him.

Colossians 3:12–17
Holy Family
Roman rite

CHILD of Bethlehem—
house of bread;
Man of Jerusalem—
city of peace;
you have loved us
without limit or condition;
in our greatness and in our misery,
in our folly and in our virtue;
may your hand be always upon us
and may your heart be within us
so that we too
may become bread and peace
for one another.

John Hammond, OSB

G OD, our Father,
you are the guardian and guide of our lives.
Your word is joy,
your will is life,
your commands bring peace.

Watch over and guide us
as you did your Son's earthly family.

Through the celebration of this feast
help us to respond to your word and will,
that we may grow together as people of faith
Contemporary   and enjoy the peace of your Kingdom.

S IMEON blessed them and said to Mary his mother: "This child is destined to be the downfall and rise of many in Israel, a sign that will be opposed—and you yourself shall be pierced with a sword—so that the thoughts of many hearts may be laid bare."

There was also a certain prophetess, Anna by name, daughter of Phanuel of the tribe of Asher. She had seen many days, having lived seven years with her husband after her marriage and then as a widow until she was eighty-four. She was constantly in the temple, worshiping day and night in fasting and prayer. Coming on the scene at this moment, she gave thanks to God and talked about the child to all who looked forward to the deliverance of Jerusalem.

Luke 2:34–38
Holy Family
Roman rite

L ET us too stand in the Temple and hold God's Son and embrace him; and that we may deserve leave to withdraw and start on our way towards a better land, let us pray to God, the all-powerful, and to the little Jesus himself, whom we so much want to speak to and hold in our arms.

His are glory and power now and always. Amen.

Origen
Third century

A FTER Jesus' birth in Bethlehem of Judea during the reign of King Herod, astrologers from the east arrived one day in Jerusalem inquiring, "Where is the newborn king of the Jews? We observed his star at its rising and have come to pay him homage." At this news King Herod became greatly disturbed, and with him all Jerusalem. Summoning all of the chief priests and scribes of the people, he inquired of them where the Messiah was to be born. "In Bethlehem of Judea," they informed him. "Here is what the prophet has written:

'And you, Bethlehem, land of Judah,
are by no means least among the princes of Judah,
since from you shall come a ruler
who is to shepherd my people Israel.'"

Herod called the astrologers aside and found out from them the exact time of the star's appearance. Then he sent them to Bethlehem, after having instructed them: "Go and get detailed information about the child. When you have discovered something, report your findings to me so that I may go and offer him homage too."

After their audience with the king, they set out. The star which they had observed at its rising went ahead of them until it came to a standstill over the place where the child was. They were overjoyed at seeing the star, and on entering the house, found the child with Mary his mother. They prostrated themselves and did him homage. Then they opened their coffers and presented him with gifts of gold, frankincense, and myrrh.

They received a message in a dream not to return to Herod, so they went back to their own country by another route.

After the astrologers had left, the angel of the Lord suddenly appeared in a dream to Joseph with the command: "Get up, take the child and his mother, and flee to Egypt. Stay there until I tell you otherwise. Herod is searching for the child to destroy him." Joseph got up and took the child and mother and left that night for Egypt. He stayed there until the death of Herod, to fulfill what the Lord had said through the prophet:

"Out of Egypt I have called my son."

Once Herod realized that he had been deceived by the astrologers, he became furious. He ordered the massacre of all the boys two years old and under in Bethlehem and its environs, making his calculation on the basis of the date he had learned from the astrologers. What was said through Jeremiah the prophet was then fulfilled:

"A cry was heard at Ramah,
   sobbing and loud lamentation:
Rachel bewailing her children;
   no comfort for her, since they are no more."

But after Herod's death, the angel of the Lord appeared in a dream to Joseph in Egypt with the command: "Get up, take the child and his mother, and set out for the land of Israel. Those who had designs on the life of the child are dead." He got up, took the child and his mother, and returned to the land of Israel. He heard, however, that Archelaus had succeeded his father Herod as king of Judea, and he was afraid to go back there. Instead, because of a warning received in a dream, Joseph went to the region of Galilee. There he settled in a town called Nazareth. In this way what was said through the prophets was fulfilled:

"He shall be called a Nazorean."

Matthew 2
Holy Innocents
Holy Family
Epiphany
Roman rite

FROM the countries of the east
came an ass,
handsome and extremely strong,
fit for burdens.
Hey, sir Ass!

He was brought up in the hills around
Sychen, in the country of the Rubenites,
leapt across the Jordan,
and sprang into Bethlehem.
Hey, sir Ass!

He jumps higher than mules,
than does, than antelopes;
he is swifter than the camels
of Madiana.
Hey, sir Ass!

As he bears the wagons,
together with many parcels,
his jaws are munching
tough fodder.
Hey, sir Ass!

He eats corn,
and also barley and thistles;
he separates the wheat
from the chaff on the threshing floor.
Hey, sir Ass!

Say Amen, Ass,
now that you are full:
again, Amen, Amen!
Away with all the past!
Hey! Hey! Hey!

The Play of Herod
Thirteenth century

Load up, sir Ass—time to go.
Sweetly now, time to sing.

H AIL, holy Mother! The child to whom you gave birth
is the King of heaven and earth for ever.

Mary, Mother of God
Roman rite

F ATHER,
source of light in every age,
the virgin conceived and bore your Son
who is called Wonderful God, Prince of Peace.
May her prayer, the gift of a mother's love,
be your people's joy through all ages.
May her response, born of a humble heart,
draw your Spirit to rest on your people.

Alternative opening
prayer
Mary, Mother of God
Roman rite

THE comfort that a mother can give in early life is like no other comfort that a child ever experiences before or after. The attachment, the need, the sense of identification and security inherent in maternal contact makes the female figure a sign and symbol of mercy and comfort, of relief and joy. . . .

This should be the goal of human relationships, a sharing in which needs are met with enjoyment and altruistic love of the other's development. It is no accident that the figure of mother has been a symbol of nurture and peace. Mother and child, the virgin and child, have appealed to more than just artists. Mary as mother and as Our Lady of Peace and Mercy has had a primal power on believers through the ages. We still long for our mother's care like infants crying in the night. Since the understanding of God as mother has been suppressed in Western Christian tradition, the experience of Mary as mother has been accentuated and fulfilled the ideal and symbol of maternal mercy and love. Mother of God she was named, and if Christ too is our mother, then she is grandmother to us all. The great mother has always been longed for and worshiped, but in other religions she was not always benign and loving. We are confirmed by Mary, who as a merciful mother and the handmaid of the Lord assures us that we will not be left with a deep anxiety within, or a fear of the total otherness and power beyond ourselves. Fear of the sacred and the natural awe of God has been complemented by a final mercy and reassurance.

Sidney Callahan
The Magnificat

HAIL Mary,
full of grace;
the Lord is with you,
the Holy Spirit too.
Your priests shall be robed in justice,
they that honor you shall rejoice and exult.
For David's sake, your servant, Lord,
save, Lord, your people, bless your chosen portion.

Hail to the glorious virgin,
Mary, full of grace.
The Lord is with you.
Blessed you are above all other women
and blessed is the fruit of your womb:
for he you conceived was Christ, the Son of God,
and he has redeemed our souls.

Coptic liturgy
Sixth or seventh
century

I sing of maiden
That is makeles [matchless]:
King of all kings
To her son she ches [chose].
He came al so stille
There his moder was,
As dew in Aprille
That falleth on the grass.

He came al so stille,
To his moder's bour,
As dew in Aprille
That falleth on the flowr.
He came al so stille
There his moder lay,
As dew in Aprille
That falleth on the spray.

Moder and mayden
Was never none but she:
Well may such a lady
Goddes moder be.

Anonymous
Fifteenth century

HAIL, O Trinity, holy and mystical, in answer to whose
call we have all assembled in this church of
Mary, the mother of God.
Hail Mary, Mother of God
    the whole world's treasure, commanding its
      reverence,
    lamp that will never cease to burn,
    crowning glory of the virgin state,
    mainstay of orthodox faith,
    temple that none can demolish,
    place that encompasses him whom no place
      encompasses,
    both mother and virgin.
Thanks to you, he that comes in the name of the Lord is
    called blessed in the holy gospels. Hail to you: to
    him that is not bounded by any place you have given
    a place in your holy, virginal womb.
Thanks to you, the Trinity is glorified and the cross called
    precious and given honor throughout the world.
Thanks to you the heavens rejoice, the angels and arch-
    angels keep festival, the evil spirits are put to flight.
Thanks to you the whole creation, ensnared by idolatry,
    came to the knowledge of the truth. Thanks to you,
    baptism was given to believers, and oil to make them
    glad.
Thanks to you, God's only Son shed his light on them
    that were living in darkness, in the shadow of death.
Thanks to you, the prophets prophesied and the
    apostles preached salvation to the Gentiles.
Thanks to you, the dead return to life and kings
    govern their people, for the sake of the
    Holy Trinity. . . .
The whole world therefore rejoices.

Cyril of Alexandria
Fifth century

THERE is no rose of such vertu
As is the rose that bare Jesu.
    Alleluia.

For in this rose conteined was
Heaven and earth in litel space,
    Res miranda.[1]

By that rose we may well see
There be one God in persons three,
    Pares forma.[2]

The angels sungen the shepherds to:
Gloria in excelsis Deo.
    Gaudeamus.[3]

Leave we all this werldly mirth,
And follow we this joyful birth.
    Transeamus.[4]

Anonymous
Fifteenth century

1 Marvelous thing!
2 Of equal form.
3 Let us rejoice!
4 Let us go across (from wordly to heavenly things)!

THE knot of Eve's disobedience was loosed by
the obedience of Mary.
    for what the virgin Eve had bound fast
        through unbelief,
    this did the virgin Mary set free
        through faith.

Irenaeus of Lyons
Second century

MARY treasured all these things and reflected on them in her heart. The shepherds returned, glorifying and praising God for all they had heard and seen, in accord with what had been told them.

When the eighth day arrived for his circumcision, the name Jesus was given the child, the name the angel had given him before he was conceived.

Luke 2:19–21
Mary, Mother of God
Roman rite

ALL people who have studied birth and the infant in the birth processes have concluded that it is indeed often a trauma and a frightful thing to be born. To come from the waters and safety and security of the womb into the new element of the world in which one breathes air and is severed from contact and warmth seems to be a journey which is violent and difficult for the new organism. So, too, our death is a birth into another element, another dimension, a separation from the womb of this life and the concrete ways of knowing what the earth has given us. Mother earth is hard to leave. The earliest remains of graves of primitive man reveal bodies put into the earth in the fetal position. So, too, some of the earliest religious stirrings and beliefs turned to a mother goddess to ease the transition from life to death. We may know God as mother and Christ as mother and the Spirit as mother, but the sense of Mary as mother is easier for us to grasp, having each had a mother in the flesh. Her exaltation as mother gives us hope and helps us to bear the approach of death.

Sidney Callahan
The Magnificat

Liturgy of the Hours
Roman rite

B Y your miraculous birth of the Virgin you have fulfilled the scriptures: like a gentle rain falling upon the earth you have come down to save your people. O God, we praise you.

I T is indeed right and proper, it is only fitting and what our duty requires of us, that always and everywhere we should give you thanks, holy Lord, almighty Father, eternal God, through Jesus Christ our Lord.

As we celebrate today the octave of his birth, we revere the marvels you wrought, Lord, when he was born: for she that gave him birth was a virgin mother, and he that was born of her was a child God.

No wonder was it that the heavens gave tongue, the angels rejoiced, the magi underwent a transformation, kings were seized with anxiety, and tiny children were crowned with the glory of martyrdom. He was our food, yet his mother fed him; he was the bread that came from heaven, yet he was laid in a manger like fodder, for the animals to eat devoutly.

Preface for the Octave
of Christmas
Gelasian sacramentary

There did the ox recognize its owner and the ass its master's crib: there did the people of the circumcision acknowledge him, there did the Gentiles acclaim him.

WHAT shall we present unto thee, O Christ,
For thy coming to earth for us?
Each of thy creatures brings thee a thank-offering:
The angels—singing; the heavens—a star;
The wise men—treasures; the shepherds—devotion;
The earth—a cave; the desert—a manger;
But we offer thee the virgin-mother.
O eternal God, have mercy upon us.

Orthodox liturgy

MARY wove a garment of glory and gave it to her father,
Adam, who was naked among the trees. He donned
this chaste robe and became beautiful. His wife led him to a
fall; his daughter supported him; he arose to be a hero.

Ephraem
Fourth century

GRACE-FILLED, unspotted, God-bearing virgin,
holy your womb: Emmanuel lay in it.
You fed at your breast the food of the world.
What praise can reach you, what glory touch you?
Hail, God's mother, delight of the angels;
hail, full of grace, foretold by prophets' preaching.
The Lord is with you. The child you bore has saved the
    world.

Early Christian prayer

O pure and holy Virgin,
 how can I find words to praise your beauty?
The highest heavens cannot contain God whom you
carried in your womb.

Blessed are you among women,
and blessed is the fruit of your womb.
Office of Readings
Liturgy of the Hours
Roman rite
The highest heavens cannot contain God whom you
carried in your womb.

G OD, bless to me the new day,
 Never vouchsafed to me before;
It is to bless thine own presence
Thou hast given me this time, O God.

Bless thou to me mine eye,
May mine eye bless all it sees;
I will bless my neighbor,
May my neighbor bless me.

God, give me a clean heart,
Let me not from sight of thine eye;
The Blessing of
the New Year
Scottish
Bless to me my children and my wife,
And bless to me my means and my cattle.

O Lord, our loving God, we thank thee that thou remainest the same and that thy years have no end; that it is thy will and thy gift to grant us to remain; that thy word remains, in which thy heart is manifest to us and which speaks to our hearts. Give us the freedom, where all else decays, to hold to it and it alone.

And now grant that in this freedom we may take today our final steps in the old year and tomorrow our first in the new, and then all further steps into that future which is granted to us, whether it be long or short.

Awaken to this same freedom and enlighten in every place more and more men and women, old and young, high and low, wise and foolish, that they too may become witnesses of that which abides forever. Let a little, or even at times much, of that dawn of eternity shine into the prisons in all lands, into the clinics and schools, the council halls and editorial rooms, into all places where humankind suffers and achieves, speaks and makes decisions, and so easily forgets that thou art the sovereign ruler and that they must answer to thee. And let such dawn shine too into the hearts and lives of our families at home, and of those many known and unknown to us who are poor, forsaken, confused, hungering, sick, and dying. And do not withhold it from us when our hour shall strike.

Mighty God, we praise thy name. In thee alone we hope, O let us not be lost. Amen.   Karl Barth

I F you consider the holiness that is God's,
you can be sure that everyone who acts in holiness
   has been begotten by him.

See what love the Father has bestowed on us
   in letting us be called children of God!
Yet that is what we are.

The reason the world does not recognize us
   is that it never recognized the Son.
Dearly beloved,
   we are God's children now;
   what we shall later be has not yet come to light.
We know that when it comes to light
   we shall be like him,
   for we shall see him as he is.
Everyone who has this hope based on him
   keeps himself pure, as he is pure.
Everyone who sins acts lawlessly,
   for sin is lawlessness.
You know well that the reason he revealed himself
   was to take away sins;
   in him there is nothing sinful.

1 John 2:29–3:6
January 3
Roman rite

The man who remains in him does not sin.
The man who sins has not seen him nor known him.

GOD our Father,
when your Son was born of the Virgin Mary
he became like us in all things but sin.
May we who have been reborn in him
be free from our sinful ways.

Liturgy of the Hours
Roman rite

BY nature we deserved God's wrath like the rest. But
God is rich in mercy; because of his great love for us he
brought us to life with Christ when we were dead in sin. By
this favor you were saved.

Ephesians 2:3b–5
Evening Prayer
December 28
Roman rite

THE Word was made [flesh]; full of grace and truth, he
lived among us. From his fullness we all have received
gift upon gift of his love, alleluia.

Morning Prayer
Tuesday from January 2
to Epiphany
Roman rite

WISDOM sings her own praises,
    before her own people she proclaims her glory;
In the assembly of the Most High she opens her mouth,
    in the presence of his hosts she declares her worth:
"From the mouth of the Most High I came forth,
    and mistlike covered the earth.
In the highest heavens did I dwell,
    my throne on a pillar of cloud.

"Then the Creator of all gave me his command,
    and he who formed me chose the spot for my tent,
Saying, 'In Jacob make your dwelling,
    in Israel your inheritance.'
Before all ages, in the beginning, he created me,
    and through all ages I shall not cease to be.
In the holy tent I ministered before him,
    and in Zion I fixed my abode.
Thus in the chosen city he has given me rest,
    in Jerusalem is my domain.
I have struck root among the glorious people,
    in the portion of the Lord, his heritage."

Sirach 24:1-4, 8-12
Second Sunday
after Christmas
Roman rite

WHEN peaceful silence lay over all, and the night had
    run half of her swift course, your all-powerful word,
O Lord, leaped down from heaven, from the royal throne.

Second Sunday
after Christmas
Roman rite

FATHER of our Lord Jesus Christ,
our glory is to stand before the world
as your own sons and daughters.
May the simple beauty of Jesus' birth
summon us always to love what is most deeply human,
and to see your Word made flesh
reflected in those whose lives we touch.

Second Sunday
after Christmas
Roman rite

CHRIST speaks both in us and for us when, in one of the psalms, he says to the Father: I shall be satisfied when your glory is revealed. For he and the Father are one, and whoever sees him sees the Father also. . . . He will transform us and show us his face, and we shall be saved; all our longing will be fulfilled, all our desires will be satisfied.

But this has not yet been accomplished. . . . So while all this remains in the future and we still walk by faith, absent from the Lord, while we still hunger and thirst for justice and with inexpressible longing yearn for God's beauty, let us reverently celebrate the day he was born into our own servile condition.

Since we can as yet form no conception of his generation by the Father before the daystar, let us keep the festival of his birth of a virgin in the hours of the night. Since it is still beyond our understanding that his name endures for ever and existed before the sun, let us at least recognize his dwelling that he has placed beneath the sun. We cannot yet behold him as the only Son, abiding for ever in his Father, so let us recall his coming forth like a bridegroom from his chamber. We are not yet ready for the banquet of our Father, so let us contemplate the manger of Jesus Christ our Lord.

Augustine
Fifth century
Office of Readings
Thursday from
January 2 to Epiphany
Roman rite

Traditional collect
for Second Sunday
after Christmas Day
*The Book of
Common Prayer*

O GOD, who didst wonderfully create, and yet more wonderfully restore, the dignity of human nature: Grant that we may share the divine life of him who humbled himself to share in our humanity, thy Son Jesus Christ.

Colossians 1:13–15
Evening Prayer
Monday from
January 2 to Epiphany
Roman rite

G OD rescued us from the power of darkness and brought us into the kingdom of his beloved Son. Through him we have redemption, the forgiveness of our sins. He is the image of the invisible God, the first-born of all creatures.

Zechariah 8:7–8
Midafternoon Prayer
Wednesday from
January 2 to Epiphany
Roman rite

L O, I will rescue my people from the land of the setting sun. I will bring them back to dwell within Jerusalem. They shall be my people, and I will be their God, with faithfulness and justice.

Revelation 21:23–24
Daytime Prayer
Monday from
January 2 to Epiphany
Roman rite

T HE city had no need of sun or moon, for the glory of God gave it light, and its lamp was the Lamb. The nations shall walk by its light; to it the kings of the earth shall bring their treasures.

FATHER, all-powerful and ever-living God, we do well
always and everywhere to give you thanks.

Today you revealed in Christ your eternal plan of salvation
and showed him as the light of all peoples.
Now that his glory has shone among us
you have renewed humanity in his immortal image.

Epiphany
Roman rite

EGERIA, a nun from Spain who visited the Holy Land about
385, found that the Nativity of Christ was celebrated in
Bethlehem with a nocturnal vigil and a eucharist on January
5–6. Unfortunately, the leaves in her diary which describe
the service have been lost, and we can only pick up her nar-
rative at the point where she was in the procession accompanying the bishop back to Jerusalem on the morning of the
Epiphany. She tells us, however, that "in Bethlehem through
the entire eight days the feast is celebrated in festal array and
joyfulness by the priests and all the clerics there and the
monks who are stationed in that place."

When Jerome settled in Bethlehem in 386 he brought with
him the Roman custom of celebrating the Nativity of Christ
on December 25. . . . But in spite of the presence of wester-
ners like Jerome, Jerusalem followed Alexandria in not
immediately copying the feast of December 25. The Armenian Lectionary, which reflects the use of the church in
Jerusalem a hundred years after Egeria's pilgrimage, men-

tions casually that "in other towns is kept the Nativity of Christ" but that in the Holy City December 25 is a commemoration of "James and David." It was not until the second half of the sixth century that Christmas Day was observed John Gunstone   there.

THE Epiphany . . . is the true "Festival of Lights," the name given to it by St. Gregory Nazianzen as far back as the fourth century. Various explanations for the name have been proposed, none entirely convincing. It would seem that once again we have to look to Egypt. . . . The description of the Coptic celebration of the Epiphany given by Al-Maqrizi, ten centuries later, shows how faithfully these customs had been preserved. He calls it the feast of the Immersion or Baptism (*Denh*):

> This feast is celebrated in Egypt on the eleventh day of the month of Tuba. The origin of the feast is that Yahia ben Zakaria (John son of Zachary), blessed be he, whom the Christians call John the Baptist, baptized the Christ, that is washed him in the lake of Jordan. And when the Christ, blessed be he, emerged from the water, the Holy Spirit came down upon him. This is why the Christians immerse their children and themselves in water on that date. This ceremony always takes place at the coldest time of the year. It is called the feast of the Immersion, and was formerly celebrated with the greatest solemnity. Al-Massoudi (in 942) describes it in these terms. . . . : The night of the Immersion was a very great feast for the inhabitants of Misr (old Cairo). No one went to bed that

night. It was the night of the eleventh day of Tuba. Mohammad ibn-Toghj l'Ikchid was in his palace in Misr, built on an island surrounded by the Nile. He caused a thousand torches to be lit by the people of Misr. There were thousands of people there on the banks of the Nile that night, Moslems and Christians, the former in boats, the latter in houses along both banks of the Nile. Nothing that could make a show was omitted: food, drink, clothes, gold and silver musical instruments, jewels and trinkets, music and good cheer. It was the greatest night Misr had ever seen, the night of most pleasure. The roads were not closed that night. Most of those present immersed themselves in the Nile; they claim this is a safeguard against bodily ailments as well as a talisman against sickness.

Irenee-Henri Dalmais

TODAY the Bridegroom claims his bride, the church, since Christ has washed her sins away in Jordan's waters; the magi hasten with their gifts to the royal wedding; and the wedding guests rejoice, for Christ has changed water into wine, alleluia.

Morning Prayer
Roman rite

THE wise men opened their treasures and offered to the Lord gifts of gold, frankincense and myrrh, alleluia.

Antiphons
Morning Prayer
Roman rite

Mighty seas and rivers, bless the Lord; springs of water, sing his praises, alleluia.

IN choosing to be born for us, God chose to be known by us. He therefore reveals himself in this way, in order that this great sacrament of his love may not be an occasion for us of great misunderstanding.

Today the magi find, crying in a manger, the one they have followed as he shone in the sky. Today the magi see clearly, in swaddling clothes, the one they have long awaited as he lay hidden among the stars.

Today the magi gaze in deep wonder at what they see: heaven on earth, earth in heaven, humanity in God, God in humanity, one whom the whole universe cannot contain now enclosed in a tiny body. As they look, they believe and do not question, as their symbolic gifts bear witness: incense for God, gold for a king, myrrh for one who is to die. . . .

Today Christ enters the Jordan to wash away the sin of the world. John himself testifies that this is why he has come: Behold the Lamb of God, behold him who takes away the sins of the world. . . .

Today Christ works the first of his signs from heaven by turning water into wine. But water [mixed with wine] has still to be changed into the sacrament of his blood, so that Christ may offer spiritual drink from the chalice of his body.

Peter Chrysologus
Fifth century
Office of Readings
Roman rite

B EGOTTEN of the Father before the daystar shone or time began, the Lord our Savior has appeared on earth today.

Evening Prayer I
Roman rite

O God, who by the leading of a star didst manifest thy only-begotten Son to the peoples of the earth: Lead us, who know thee now by faith, to thy presence, where we may behold thy glory face to face.

Collect for Epiphany
The Book of
Common Prayer

T HE star was a particularly evocative symbol. Variously interpreted as a figure of an angel or as a sign of the Holy Spirit, it pointed the magi (and so also the members of the church who meditate on the gospel) to Christ.

"Is it to be wondered at," asked John Chrysostom, "that a divine star ministers to the rising Sun of Righteousness? It halts above the head of the child as if saying, 'This is he.'"

John Gunstone

Collect for Second
Sunday after the
Epiphany
*The Book of
Common Prayer*

ALMIGHTY God, whose Son our Savior Jesus Christ is the light of the world: Grant that thy people, illumined by thy Word and Sacraments, may shine with the radiance of Christ's glory, that he may be known, worshiped, and obeyed to the ends of the earth.

Ignatius of Antioch
Second century

A star burned in the sky more brightly than all the others; its light was indescribable, its newness marvelous, and all the other stars, along with the sun and the moon, formed a chorus around this star, the light of which reached farther than that of any other. . . . Then all magic was destroyed, and every bond wrought by wickedness was broken, and the ancient kingdom was razed. When God appeared in human form to bring the newness of eternal life, his counsel began to be fulfilled.

RISE up in splendor, Jerusalem! your light has come,
the glory of the Lord shines upon you.
See, darkness covers the peoples;
But upon you the Lord shines,
   and over you appears his glory.
Nations shall walk by your light,
   and kings by your shining radiance.
Raise your eyes and look about;
   they all gather and come to you:
Your sons come from afar,
   and your daughters in the arms of their nurses.
Then you shall be radiant at what you see,
   your heart shall throb and overflow,
For the riches of the sea shall be emptied out before you,
   the wealth of nations shall be brought to you.
Caravans of camels shall fill you,
   dromedaries from Midian and Ephah;
All from Sheba shall come
   bearing gold and frankincense,
   and proclaiming the praises of the Lord.

Isaiah 60:1–6
Roman rite

THE loving providence of God determined that in the last days he would aid the world, set on its course to destruction. He decreed that all nations should be saved in Christ. . . .

Let the full number of the nations now take their place in the family of the patriarchs. Let the children of the promise now receive the blessing in the seed of Abraham. . . . In the persons of the magi let all people adore the creator of the universe; let God be known, not in Judea only, but in the whole world, so that *his name may be great in all Israel*.

Dear friends, now that we have received instruction in this revelation of God's grace, let us celebrate with spiritual joy the day of our first harvesting, of the first calling of the Gentiles. Let us give thanks to the merciful God, *who has made us worthy, in the words of the Apostle, to share the position of the saints in light; who has rescued us from the power of darkness, and brought us into the kingdom of his beloved Son*. As Isaiah prophesied: *The people of the Gentiles, who sat in darkness, have seen a great light, and for those who dwelt in the region of the shadow of death a light has dawned. He spoke of them to the Lord: The Gentiles, who do not know you, will invoke you, and the people, who knew you not, will take refuge in you*. . . .

This came to be fulfilled, as we know, from the time when the star beckoned the three wise men out of their distant country and led them to recognize and adore the king of heaven and earth. The obedience of the star calls us to imitate its humble service: to be servants, as best we can, of the grace that invites us all to find Christ.

Leo the Great
Fifth century
Office of Readings
Roman rite

ONLY a few days ago we celebrated the Lord's birthday. Today we are celebrating with equal solemnity, as is proper, his Epiphany, in which he began to manifest himself to the Gentiles. On the one day the Jewish shepherds saw him when he was born; on this day the magi coming from the east adored him. Now, he had been born that cornerstone, the peace of the two walls coming from very different directions, from circumcision and uncircumcision. Thus they could be united in him who had been made our peace, and "who has made both one." This was foretokened in the Jewish shepherds and the Gentile magi. From this began what was to grow and to bear fruit throughout the world. Let us, therefore, with joy of the spirit hold dear these two days, the Nativity and the Manifestation of our Lord. The Jewish shepherds were led by an angel bringing the news; the Gentile magi by a star showing the way.

Augustine
Fifth century

O God, with your judgment endow the king,
   and with your justice, the king's son;
He shall govern your people with justice
   and your afflicted ones with judgment.
The mountains shall yield peace for the people,
   and the hills justice.
He shall defend the afflicted among the people,
   save the children of the poor,
   and crush the oppressor.
May he endure as long as the sun,
   and like the moon through all generations.
He shall be like rain coming down on the meadow,
   like showers watering the earth.
Justice shall flower in his days,
   and profound peace, till the moon be no more.

May he rule from sea to sea,
   and from the River to the ends of the earth.
His foes shall bow before him,
   and his enemies shall lick the dust.
The kings of Tarshish and the Isles shall offer gifts;
   the kings of Arabia and Seba shall bring tribute.
All kings shall pay him homage,
   all nations shall serve him.

For he shall rescue the poor man when he cries out,
   and the afflicted when he has no one to help him.
He shall have pity for the lowly and the poor;
   the lives of the poor he shall save.
From fraud and violence he shall redeem them,
   and precious shall their blood be in his sight.

May he live to be given the gold of Arabia,
   and to be prayed for continually;
   day by day shall they bless him.

May there be an abundance of grain upon the earth;
   on the tops of the mountains the crops shall rustle
      like Lebanon;
   the city dwellers shall flourish like the verdure of the
      fields.
May his name be blessed forever;
   as long as the sun his name shall remain.
In him shall all the tribes of the earth be blessed;
   all the nations shall proclaim his happiness.

Blessed be the LORD, the God of Israel,
   who alone does wondrous deeds.
And blessed forever be his glorious name;
   may the whole earth be filled with his glory.
   Amen. Amen.   Psalm 72

As with gladness men of old,
Did the guiding star behold,
As with joy they hailed its light,
Leading onwards beaming bright,
So, most gracious God, may we
Evermore be led to thee.

As with joyful steps they sped
To that lowly manger-bed,
There to bend the knee before
Him whom heaven and earth adore,
So may we with willing feet
Ever seek thy mercy-seat.

As they offered gifts most rare
At that manger rude and bare,
So may we with holy joy,
Pure, and free from sin's alloy,
All our costliest treasures bring,
Christ, to thee our heavenly king.

Holy Jesus, every day
Keep us in the narrow way;
And, when earthly things are past,
Bring our ransomed souls at last
Where they need no star to guide,
Where no clouds thy glory hide.

In the heavenly country bright
Need they no created light;
Thou its light, its joy, its crown,
Thou its sun which goes not down:
There for ever may we sing
Alleluias to our king.

W. Chatterton Dix
Nineteenth century

I am sure you have heard of the ministry which God in his goodness gave me in your regard. God's secret plan, as I have briefly described it, was revealed to me, unknown in former ages but now revealed by the Spirit to the holy apostles and prophets. It is no less than this: in Christ Jesus the Gentiles are now co-heirs with the Jews, members of the same body and sharers of the promise through the preaching of the gospel.

Ephesians 3:2–3, 5–6
Roman rite

THE gifts of God are multiplied, and we in our time experience all that the first believers did. For though the gospel account tells us only of the days when three men, untaught by prophetic preaching or the testimonies of the Law, came from the distant East in order to know God, yet we see the same thing happening now even more clearly and on a far larger scale in the enlightenment of all who are called.

Leo the Great
Fifth century

P RAISE the Lord, all you nations.

Christ manifested in the flesh,
Christ justified in the Spirit.

Praise the Lord, all you nations.

Christ contemplated by the angels,
Christ proclaimed by the pagans.

Praise the Lord, all you nations.

Canticle based on
1 Timothy 3:16
Evening Prayer I
Roman rite

Christ who is believed in the world,
Christ exalted in glory.

Praise the Lord, all you nations.

EXALTED King, what hast thou to do with lowly ones?
    Creator of heaven, why hast thou come to men on
        earth?
Didst thou long for the cave, or joy in the manger?
Lo, there is no place for thy handmaiden at the inn;
    There is no place, not even a cave,
    Since that, too, belongs to another.
On Sarah, as she was to bring forth a child,
Was bestowed a great inheritance of land, but to me,
    Not even a den.
I made use of the cave in which thou didst will
        to dwell as
            A newborn babe, the God before time.

While she was pondering these things in secret,
    And entreating him who has knowledge of all secret
        things,
    She hears the magi who are seeking the child.
Straightway, the maiden called out to them: ''Who are
        you?''
    And they to her: ''Who art thou
    Who hast produced and brought forth such a one?
Who, thy father? Who, thy mother?
    For thou hast become the mother and nurse of a
        fatherless son.
It was his star that we saw when we came to behold
        A newborn babe, the God before time.''

''Clearly did Balaam reveal to us
    The meaning of the words which were prophesied,
    Saying that a star would rise up,
A star which would dim all prophecies and divination,
    A star to destroy the parables of the wise,
    Their teachings and their enigmas,
A star much brighter than this star which just appeared,

For he is the maker of stars
About whom it was written: 'From Jacob shall rise up
    A newborn babe, the God before time.'"

When Mary heard the words of wonder,
    She knelt in obeisance to the one from her womb,
Mary   And crying out, she said: "Great things, my child,
Great are all the things which thou hast done for
    My humble station;
    For lo, the magi without are seeking thee;
Those who are kings of the east
    Seek thy presence,
And the wealthy of thy people beg to behold thee;
For truly the people are thine. They are the ones for
    whom thou wast known as
        A newborn babe, the God before time.

Mary "Since the people are thine, my child, bid them
    to come beneath this roof that they may see
    A poverty full of plenty, and beggary which is
    honored.
I consider thee a glory and cause for boast, so that I am
    not ashamed.
    Thou, thyself, art the grace and the comeliness
    Of my dwelling. Bid them enter.
To me the want is no concern,
    For I consider thee as a treasure which the kings came
    to see;
For the kings and the magi know that thou hast
    appeared as
        A newborn babe, the God before time."

Jesus Christ, who is truly our God.
    Secretly suggested to his mother:
Christ   "Admit them, for my word led them,
And shone on those who were seeking me.

To all appearances, it is a star;
But in reality, it is a power.
It went with the magi in service to me;
And still it stands outside fulfilling its ministry,
And revealing with its beams the place where there has
been born,
A newborn babe, the God before time.

st   "Now receive, revered one, receive those who received
me;
For I am in them as I am in thy arms,
Nor was I away from thee when I accompanied them."
She, then, opens the door, she who is the unopened gate
Through which Christ alone passed;
She opens the door, she who was opened
And never gave up the treasure of her virginity;
She opened the door, she, from whom was born the
door,
A newborn babe, the God before time.

Romanos
Sixth century

BEHOLD kings have come, that they might adore the heavenly king of glory; soldiers, that they might serve the leader of the hosts of heaven; women, that they might adore him who was born of a woman so that he might change the pains of childbirth into joy; virgins, to the son of the Virgin, beholding with joy, that he who is the giver of milk, who has decreed that the fountains of the breast pour forth in ready streams, receives from a virgin mother the food of infancy; infants, that they may adore him who became a little child, so *that out of the mouth of infants and of sucklings*, he might perfect praise; children, to the child who raised up martyrs through the rage of Herod; men, to him who became a man, that he might heal the miseries of his servants; shepherds, to the Good Shepherd who has laid down his life for his sheep; priests, to him who has become a high priest according to the order of Melchisedech; servants, to him who *took upon himself the form of a servant* that he might bless our servitude with the reward of freedom; publicans, to him who from amongst them named a chosen evangelist; sinful women, to him who exposed his feet to the tears of the repentant; and that I may embrace them all together, all sinners have come, that they may look upon the Lamb of God who taketh away the sins of the world.

Since therefore all rejoice, I too desire to rejoice. I too wish to share the choral dance, to celebrate the festival. But I take my part, not plucking the harp, not shaking the Thyrsian staff, not with the music of the pipes, nor holding a torch, but holding in my arms the cradle of Christ. For this is all my hope, this my life, this my salvation, this my pipe, my harp. And bearing it I come, and having from its power received the gift of speech, I too, with the angels, sing: *Glory to God in the Highest*; and with the shepherds, *and on earth peace to men of good will*.

John Chrysostom
Fifth century

M OST of the traditional holidays of Christendom have become awkward occasions, and a few of the great Christian festivals have been taken over so completely by commercialism that their degeneracy is almost total.

But this is not the whole picture. In this same contemporary world of ours there remains the indestructible (for otherwise human nature itself would have to be destroyed) gift innate in all humans which impels them now and again to escape from the restricted sphere where they labor for their necessities and provide for their security—to escape not by mere forgetting, but by undeceived recollection of the greater, more real reality. Now, as always, the workaday world can be transcended in poetry and the other arts. In the shattering emotion of love, beyond the delusions of sensuality, we continue to find entrance to the still point of the turning world. Now, as always, the experience of death as our destiny, if accepted with an open and unarmored heart, acquaints us with a dimension of existence which fosters a detachment from the immediate aims of practical life. Now, as always, the philosophical mind will react with awe to the mystery of being revealed in a grain of matter or a human face.

Of course, all such responses are not in themselves festivity. They are the postludes of festivity, but in the proper circumstances they could again become the preludes. All such modes of ascending out of the world of mere utility once arose from the soil of a festival perhaps long since faded or forgotten; and so they may, by virtue of their evocative power, once again become a step toward a new festival to be celebrated in the future.

The core and source of festivity itself remains inviolably present in the midst of society. This is as true today as it was a thousand years ago. It remains in the form of the praise given in ritual worship, which is literally performed at every hour of the day. By its nature that praise is a public act, a festival celebrated before the face of Creation, whether its site is a catacomb or a prisoner's cell. And because the festive occasion pure and simple, the divine guarantee of the world and of human salvation, exists and remains true continuously, we may say that in essence one single everlasting festival is being celebrated—so that the distinction between holiday and workday appears to be quite erased.

Josef Pieper
In Tune with the World

B Y this they knew him: that he, like them, was marked
for death;
and, knowing this, they knew themselves no longer
strangers.
They fell down before him and offered gifts,
gold and frankincense and myrrh,
the wealth of nations laid at his feet,
nothing held back.
They had observed his star at its rising and had come to
pay him homage.
In facing death they had arrived.
Before this child marked for death
they were no longer fugitives and strangers.
In the presence of this child
they were at home.

In this city, we are mostly strangers:
strangers as much to its glitter as to its degradation,
strangers to its power and its powerless,
gawking spectators of its opulence.

Ill-at-ease amid its ghettos, its violence, its profanity.
Faces flash by us on the street, "tired of wishes, emptied
    of dreams,"
everyone a stranger, never seen before nor since.
And yet, each a face, a life, a history for whom the Christ
    was born
and whose image he held in mind in the hour of his
    dying.

In this strange land, amid these unfamiliar faces,
there is a way to see the Epiphany:
the way of the magi, of the strangers who came in from
    the night.
It is to see ourselves and to recognize our condition
in these otherwise alien people.
It is to know ourselves compacted with them in a
    common destiny,
the destiny of children marked for death,
heirs of the promise through the Child marked for death.

Before such mutual recognition, all estrangement pales.
Whatever our differences in life, we are bound together
    in death:
that is our common lot.
And this is the promise we rejoice in with them:
that with them we are co-heirs of life in Jesus Christ,
the Child marked for death.

What is assumed by him, the Fathers say, is redeemed
    for us.
Our mortality becomes the door to immortality,

since this Immortal One was born mortal
with us and for us.
What is assumed is redeemed:
but whatever he took on himself we must ourselves
    take up.
Knowing we share the same curse and the same promise
as the Jews and the Puerto Ricans,
the shop-girls and the porn-peddlers,
Marshall Field and the city cop,
the lady swathed in fur and the women and children
    marked by wanton hunger,
in knowing ourselves co-heirs with them, members of
    the same Body,
we know the Child the wise men found with Mary his
    mother,
the Child marked to die.

We observed his star at its rising and have come to pay
    him homage:
Mark Searle   to proclaim his death until he comes in glory.

B Y bowing your head before the Precursor you crushed
the heads of the demons; you stood amid the waters and
Vespers   enlightened the universe so that it might glorify you, O
Byzantine rite   Savior, enlightener of our souls.

THE Lord went down today into the waters of the Jordan
and said to John: "Do not be afraid to baptize me, for I
have come to save Adam, the first father."   Byzantine rite

TODAY thou hast appeared to the world
And thy light, O Lord, has been a sign to us
With the full knowledge of those who sing hymns
        to thee
            Thou hast come, thou hast appeared,
            O light unapproachable.

In the Galilee of nations, in the country of Zebulun and
        in the land of the Naphthali,
    Christ, a great light, has shone forth, as the prophet
        said.
    For those in darkness, a shining light has been seen,
        sending its beams from Bethlehem;
Or rather, Christ, born of Mary, the sun of righteousness,
        Sends forth rays of light to the world.
Hither, then, all naked sons of Adam,
        Let us clothe him again that we may be warmed.
As covering for the naked, as light for those in darkness,
            Thou hast come, thou hast appeared,
            O light unapproachable.

God did not despise the one who, in paradise, was
        tricked by guile

And despoiled of the robe which God had woven for
him.
Again he has come to him, calling with holy voice the
one who was misled:
"Where art thou, Adam? This time do not hide from me;
I wish to see you.
Even if you are naked and poor, do not be ashamed,
for I am fashioned like you.
Even though you desired it, you did not become God;
But I now have willed it and become flesh.
Draw near to me and recognize me so that you may say:
'Thou hast come, thou hast appeared,
O light unapproachable.'

"Overcome by feelings of pity, I, the merciful, have
come to my creature,
Holding out my hands that I may embrace you.
Do not feel shame before me; it is for you who are
naked that I became naked and came to be
baptized.
Now the Jordan is opened for me, and John
Prepares the way for me in the water and in the hearts
of men."
Having thus addressed the man—in deed, not in words—
The Savior came, as he had said,
Directing his footsteps near the river, he appeared
To the Forerunner
As the unapproachable light.

Romanos
Sixth century

READINGS FOR THE FEAST OF THE THEOPHANY IN THE ORTHODOX LITURGY

GREAT VESPERS

Genesis 1:1–13	The spirit hovers over the waters.
Exodus 14:15–18, 21–23, 27–29	Crossing the waters to freedom.
Exodus 15:22–16:1	Making the bitter waters sweet.
Joshua 3:7–8, 15–17	Crossing the Jordan.
2 Kings 2:9–14	Elijah strikes the Jordan.
Isaiah 1:16–20	Wash yourselves clean.
Genesis 32:1–10	Jacob returns to cross the Jordan.
Exodus 2:5–10,	Pharaoh's daughter takes Moses from the water.
Judges 6:36–40	The dew a sign of God's intent to save Israel.
1 Kings 18:30–39	Elijah fills the trench with water and calls on the Lord.
2 Kings 2:19–22	Elisha purifies the water.
Isaiah 49:8–15	They shall not hunger or thirst.

NEW TESTAMENT READINGS AT THE ROYAL HOURS

Acts 13:25–33	Paul preaches about the Baptist.
Mark 3:1–6	John's preaching.
Acts 19:1–8	Baptism in the Holy Spirit.
Mark 1:1–8	John's baptism of repentance.
Romans 6:3–11	Our baptism is baptism into his death.
Mark 1:9–11	The baptism of Jesus.
Titus 2:11–14, 3:4–7	To cleanse a people.
Matthew 3:13–17 or Luke 3:1–18	The baptism of Jesus.

THE DIVINE LITURGY

1 Corinthians 9:19–27	The universality of salvation.
Luke 3:1–18	The baptism of Jesus.

THE BLESSING OF THE WATER

Isaiah 35:1–10	Streams will burst forth in the desert.
Isaiah 12:3–6	Draw water at the fountain of salvation.
Isaiah 55:1–13	All who are thirsty, come to the water.
1 Corinthians 10:1–4	Our ancestors all passed through the sea.
Mark 1:9–11	The baptism of Jesus.

BEHOLD, your God will come with vengeance, with the recompense of God. He will come and save you. Then the eyes of the blind shall be opened, and the ears of the deaf unstopped; then shall the lame man leap like a hart, and the tongue of the dumb sing for joy. For waters shall break forth in the wilderness, and streams in the desert; the burning sand shall become a pool, and the thirsty ground springs of water. And a highway shall be there, and it shall be called the Holy Way; the unclean shall not pass over it, and fools shall not enter therein. No lion shall be there, nor shall any ravenous beast come up on it; they shall not be found there, but the redeemed shall walk there.

Isaiah 35:4–7a, 8–9
Byzantine rite

ETERNAL God, you revealed yourself from heaven in the sound of thunder over the river Jordan in order to make known the Savior of the world and show yourself the Father of eternal light. You opened the heavens, blessed the air, purified the water-springs, and pointed out your only Son by sending the Holy Spirit in the form of a dove. The fonts today received your blessing and removed the curse that lay on us, offering to believers purification from all their sins and giving them birth into eternal life as adoptive children of God.

Preface for Epiphany
Milanese liturgy

THE blessing of waters on the feast of the Epiphany is thought by some to be a Christian version of a pagan ceremony, by others to be a prebaptismal blessing. Various prayers are used in different rites:

> This day the heavens were opened, and the sea was made sweet: the earth rejoices and the mountains and hills are glad, because Christ is baptized of John in Jordan;

> The voice of the Lord crieth upon the waters, saying, "O come ye and receive ye all the Spirit of wisdom, the Spirit of understanding, the Spirit of the fear of God, even Christ, who is made manifest."

A Syriac rubric instructs the archimandrite and his attendant priests to wave a fan over "the fountain, or the well, or the pool, or the river," to symbolize the breath of the Spirit!

John Gunstone

A CCEPT from us a thanksgiving worthy of your greatness for the wonderful deeds and magnificent works you have done since the beginning of the world and especially in these last times as you effect your plan of sanctification. . . .

Today the grace of the Holy Spirit descends upon the waters in the form of a dove.
. . . Today the waters of the Jordan are changed into a
    remedy by the presence of the Lord.
. . . Today sins are wiped away in the waters of the Jordan.
. . . Today paradise is opened to us, and the Sun of Justice
    shines upon us.
. . . Today the kingdom of heaven has become ours. . . .
This is the feast of the Lord that we see today in the Jordan; we see him casting into the Jordan the death due us for our disobedience, the stinging goad of error, and the chains that bound Adam; we see him giving to the world a baptism that saves.

Prayer for blessing
the water
Armenian liturgy

A T St. Petersburg, on Epiphany, the feast of the Jordan is celebrated with great solemnity on the Neva, in front of the Czar's palace. A richly decorated chapel, open on all sides, is built, with a hole in the center of the flooring and down through the ice. At ten in the morning, the metropolitan of St. Petersburg celebrates in this temporary chapel a solemn Mass, at which all the great dignitaries of the church and the troops of the Imperial Guard are present. After the divine service, the emperor arrives with his entire court. Then the metropolitan blesses the Neva by lowering a cross in the open hole, while cannon are fired and the troops, kneeling and bareheaded, present arms. Everyone then tries to touch his lips with the water that has just been blessed and to get some of it for himself by making holes in the ice. In some provinces, the peasants make a hole in the ice in order to plunge into the water themselves; elsewhere, people are content to gather the water in containers.

The Liturgical Year
Adrian Nocent

I N the feast foregone, we have seen you as a babe, and in
the present feast we see you as a perfect man, O our
    perfect God, appearing out of perfection:
for today we have attained the time of feasting, and the
    ranks of saints have joined us, and the angels celebrate
    together with us;
today, the grace of the Holy Spirit, in the likeness of a dove,
    comes down upon the waters;
today there shines the Sun that never sets, and the world is
    sparkling with the light of the Lord;
today the moon is bright, together with the earth, in the
    glowing radiance of its beams;
today the brilliant stars adorn the universe with the
    splendor of their twinkling;
today the clouds from heaven shed upon us a shower
    of justice;
today the Uncreated One willingly permits the hands of his
    creature to be laid upon him;
today the Prophet and Forerunner comes close to the
    Master, and he stands in awe, a witness of the
    condescension of God towards us;
today through the presence of the Lord the waters of the
    Jordan River are changed into remedies;
today the whole universe is refreshed with mystical streams;
today sins are blotted out by the waters of the Jordan River;
today paradise has been opened, and the Sun of
    righteousness has shone upon us;
today at the hands of Moses, the bitter water is changed
    into sweetness by the presence of the Lord;
today we are delivered from the ancient mourning, and,
    like a new Israel, we are saved;
today we escape from darkness, and, through the light of
    the knowledge of God, we are illumined;
today the darkness of the world vanishes with the

appearing of our God;
today the whole creation is brightened from on high;
today errors are cancelled, and a way of salvation is
      prepared for us by the coming of the Lord;
today the heavenly dwellers rejoice with those of the earth,
      and the dwellers of earth with those of heaven;
today the noble and eloquent assembly rejoices, the
      assembly of those of the true faith;
today the Lord comes to be baptized, so that humankind
      may be lifted up;
today the one who never has to bow inclines himself
      before his servant so that He may release our chains;
today we have acquired the kingdom of heaven: indeed,
      the kingdom of heaven that has no end.

Feast of the
Theophany [Epiphany]
Orthodox liturgy

G REAT is the Lord and marvelous are his works. No words are adequate to sing his wonders. By his being, from nothingness, he made all things. By his majesty he upholds the world, and by his providence he directs the world. When he made the universe from the four elements, he crowned the circle of the year with the four seasons. All sentient powers tremble before him.

The sun sings his praise. The moon glorifies him. The stars stand in his presence. Light obeys him. The oceans shudder with awe before him, and bubbling springs do his bidding. He has spread out the heavens like the canvas of a tent. He has established the earth upon the depths. With sand he holds back the sea.

The angels serve him. The archangels adore him. The many-eyed seraphim veil their faces before him.

He cannot be measured in any way; he cannot be described. He is from everlasting. Yet, he came down upon the earth and took the form of a slave. He was made in our likeness. He could not endure, because of his tender-hearted mercy, to see us tormented by evil. He came, and saved us. He has set us free. All creation praises him.

He has revealed himself to us. He has made himself known upon the earth, and dwelled with us. And he blessed the streams of the Jordan by sending down the Holy Spirit.

May the blessings of Jordan be upon this water! May the blessings of Jordan be upon this water! May the blessings of Jordan be upon this water!

And may we who partake of it be cleansed and purified, blessed and sanctified, healed and made whole, so that we may be filled with fullness of God who is all in all.

Adaptation of the
Great Blessing of Water
Byzantine rite

Amen! Amen! Amen!

The priest says:

I NCLINE your ear, O Lord, and hear us. O you who sanctified water when you consented to be baptized in the Jordan River: bless us all who, through the bowing of our heads, have signified our bondage, and make us worthy to be filled with your sanctification through the reception and the sprinkling of this water. Let it be, O Lord, for the health of our soul and body.

For you are the sanctification of our souls and bodies, and we send up glory, and thanksgiving, and worship, to you, O Father who have no beginning, and to your all-holy, good and life-giving Spirit, now and always and for ever and ever.
Amen.

And the priest immerses the precious cross up and down in the holy water, and recites the troparion of the Theophany:

At your baptism in the Jordan River, O Christ, the worship due to the Holy Trinity was made manifest, for the voice of the Father bore you witness by calling you "Beloved Son"; and the Holy Spirit, in the form of a dove, confirmed the immutability of this declaration. O Christ God, who appeared and filled the world with light, glory to you!

He sprinkles with the holy water all the people, and the four corners of the church, while the choir sings.

From the Blessing
of the Water
Orthodox Liturgy

B ECAUSE the liturgy celebrates events from a postpaschal perspective, the church saw in the baptism an epiphany of Christ's triumph. In scriptural thought, water symbolizes (among other things) the abode of evil. According to one tradition, which can be charted through the Psalms, Job and Isaiah, the LORD trampled on the mythical monsters of the deep, Leviathan and Rahab, the figures of evil and chaos. Stepping down into the river, therefore, Christ at his baptism stamped out the power of the devil. This is why in the oriental rites, Psalm 74 is often associated with the Epiphany: "Thou didst divide the sea through thy power: thou breakest the heads of the dragons in the waters."

John Gunstone

T HE holy day of lights, to which we have come and which we are celebrating today, has for its origin the baptism of my Christ, the true Light that lightens everyone coming into the world, and effects my purification. . . . It is a season of new birth: let us be born again! We duly celebrated at his birth—I, the one who presided at the feast, and you, and all that is in the world and above the world. With the star we ran, with the magi we worshiped, with the shepherds we were enlightened, with the angels we glorified him, with Simeon we took him up in his arms, and with the chaste and aged Anna we made our responsive confession. . . . Now we come to another of Christ's acts and another mystery. . . . The Spirit bears witness to his Godhead, for he descends upon one that is like him, as does the voice from heaven. . . . Let us venerate today the baptism of Christ.

Gregory of Nazianzus
Fourth century

THERE was a wedding at Cana in Galilee, and the mother of Jesus was there. Jesus and his disciples had likewise been invited to the celebration. At a certain point the wine ran out, and Jesus' mother told him, "They have no more wine." Jesus replied, "Woman, how does this concern of yours involve me? My hour has not yet come." His mother instructed those waiting on table, "Do whatever he tells you." As prescribed for Jewish ceremonial washings, there were at hand six stone water jars, each one holding fifteen to twenty-five gallons. "Fill those jars with water," Jesus ordered, at which they filled them to the brim. "Now," he said, "draw some out and take it to the waiter in charge." They did as he instructed them. The waiter in charge tasted the water made wine, without knowing where it had come from; only the waiters knew, since they had drawn the water. Then the waiter in charge called the groom over and remarked to him: "People usually serve the choice wine first; then when the guests have been drinking awhile, a lesser vintage. What you have done is keep the choice wine until now." Jesus performed this first of his signs at Cana in Galilee. Thus did he reveal his glory, and his disciples believed in him.

After this he went down to Capernaum, along with his mother and brothers [and his disciples] but they stayed there only a few days.

John 2:1–12
January 7
Roman rite

WHAT grace water has, before God and his Christ, for bringing out the meaning of baptism! Christ is never unaccompanied by water. He himself is baptized in water, and when he is invited to a marriage, he uses water in making his first show of power. . . . His witness to baptism continues right up to his passion.

Tertullian
Third century

HEROD, why this impiety?
Can Christ awake anxiety?
He'll let your little kingdom live
who has immortal crowns to give.

Intent upon the beckoning star,
the obedient sages followed far,
and in its light they sought the Light
and by their gifts they showed his might.

Lambent the waves the limbs adored
of heaven's Lamb, their humble Lord;
and washing him they cleansing won
for sins that we, not he, had done.

Nature beheld her usual sway
suspended in a novel way:
for water, in the Savior's name
like wine decanted, wine became.

Sedulius
Vespers hymn
Divine Office
Roman rite

G OD has called you out of darkness,
into his wonderful light.
May you experience his kindness and blessings,
and be strong in faith, in hope, and in love.

Because you are followers of Christ,
who appeared on this day as a light shining in darkness,
may he make you a light to all your sisters and brothers.

The wise men followed the star,
and found Christ who is light from light.
May you too find the Lord
when your pilgrimage is ended.

Solemn blessing
Roman rite

T HIS is the glorious day on which Christ himself, the
savior of the world, appeared;
the prophets foretold him, the angels worshiped him;
the magi saw his star and rejoiced to lay their treasures
    at his feet.
God's holy day has dawned for us at last;
come, all you peoples, and adore the Lord.

Office of Readings
Roman rite

D EAR brothers and sisters:
The glory of the Lord has shone upon us, and shall ever manifest itself among us, until the day of his return. Through the rhythms and changes of time, let us call to mind and live the mysteries of salvation.

The center of the whole liturgical year is the Paschal Triduum of the Lord, crucified, buried and risen, which will culminate in the solemn Vigil of Easter, during the holy night that will end with the dawn of the [date]. Every Sunday, as in a weekly Easter, holy church makes present that great and saving deed by which Christ has forever conquered sin and death.

From Easter there comes forth and are reckoned all the days we keep holy: Ash Wednesday, the beginning of the lenten spring, the [date]; The Ascension of the Lord, the [date]; and Pentecost, the [date]; the First Sunday of Advent, the [date].

Likewise in the feasts of the holy Mother of God, of the apostles and saints, and in the commemoration of the faithful departed, the pilgrim church on earth proclaims the resurrection of Jesus Christ our Lord.

To Christ who was, who is, and who is to come, the Lord of time and history, be endless praise forever and ever! Amen!

Epiphany proclamation

FATHER in heaven, who at the baptism of Jesus in the River
Jordan didst proclaim him thy beloved Son and anoint
him with the Holy Spirit: Grant that all who are baptized into
his Name may keep the covenant they have made, and
boldly confess him as Lord and Savior.

Collect for the
Baptism of our Lord
The Book of
Common Prayer

HERE is my servant whom I uphold,
my chosen one with whom I am pleased,
Upon whom I have put my spirit;
   he shall bring forth justice to the nations,
Not crying out, not shouting,
   not making his voice heard in the the street.
A bruised reed he shall not break,
   and a smoldering wick he shall not quench,
Until he establishes justice on the earth;
   the coastlands will wait for his teaching.

I, the Lord, have called you for the victory of
     justice,
   I have grasped you by the hand;
I formed you, and set you
   as a covenant of the people,
   a light for the nations,
To open the eyes of the blind,
   to bring out prisoners from confinement,
   and from the dungeon, those who live in darkness.

Isaiah 42:1-4, 6-7
Baptism of the Lord
Roman rite

Wᴇ are urged to move quickly beyond the intimate scene of Jesus' birth toward the more challenging vision of his baptism. In short, we are asked to move in the direction of life itself: from concern for intimacy to concern for community.

A Christian parish becomes its best self when it accepts the challenge of community. The parish community, as the real expression of a local church, cannot limit its attention to the search for justice and intimacy among its own members; it must be prepared to take up the cross, standing against evil and injustice wherever they exist in the world. This may seem like a harsh message for the Christmas season, but in fact it is the church's message at all times, in all seasons. There is, ultimately, *only one mystery* Christians celebrate: the paschal mystery, Jesus' dying and rising in a new human community called "church."

Nathan Mitchell

Tʜᴇ theme of John's preaching was: "One more powerful than I is to come after me. I am not fit to stoop and untie his sandal straps. I have baptized you in water; he will baptize you in the Holy Spirit."

During that time, Jesus came from Nazareth in Galilee and was baptized in the Jordan by John. Immediately on coming up out of the water he saw the sky rent in two and the Spirit descending on him like a dove. Then a voice came from the heavens: "You are my beloved Son. On you my favor rests."

Mark 1:7–11
Baptism of the Lord
Roman rite

THE one called "The voice crying in the wilderness"
heard your voice when you thundered upon many
   waters, Lord,
bearing witness to your Son.
Wholly filled with the Spirit that had come,
John cried aloud:
"You are Christ, the wisdom and the power of God."

"Who has ever seen the sun that is bright by nature
   being cleansed?"
"How, then, shall I wash you in the waters,
you who are the Brightness of the Glory,
the Image of the everlasting Father?
How shall I that am grass touch with my hand the fire of
   thy divinity?
For you are Christ, the wisdom and the power of God."

"Moses, when he came upon you, displayed the holy
   reverence that he felt:
perceiving that it was your voice that spoke from the
   bush,
he forthwith turned away his gaze.
How then shall I behold you openly,
how shall I lay my hand upon you?
For you are Christ, the wisdom and the power of God.

"If I baptize you,
I shall have as my accusers the mount that smoked with
   fire,
the sea which fled on either side,
and this same Jordan which turned back.
For you are Christ, the wisdom and the power of God."   Matins
                                                          Orthodox liturgy

J ESUS comes out of the water, drawing the world with him, as it were, and raising it up when it had hitherto been sunk in the abyss. He sees the heavens, not being rent, but opening of their own accord. The first Adam had of old closed heaven to himself and us, just as he had seen the earthly paradise being closed to him, with a fiery sword barring access.

The Holy Spirit bears witness. Here all is in perfect harmony, for the testimony comes from heaven, just as he to whom the Spirit bears witness has come from heaven.

Gregory of Nazianzus
Fourth century

OH, love, how deep, how broad, how high,
Beyond all thought and fantasy,
That God, the Son of God, should take
Our mortal form for mortal's sake!

He sent no angel to our race,
Of higher or of lower place,
But wore the robe of human frame,
And to this world himself he came.

For us baptized, for us he bore
His holy fast and hungered sore;
for us temptation sharp he knew;
For us the tempter overthrew.

For us he prayed; for us he taught;
For us his daily works he wrought,
By words and signs and actions thus
Still seeking not himself, but us.

For us by wickedness betrayed,
For us, in crown of thorns arrayed,
He bore the shameful cross and death;
For us he gave his dying breath.

For us he rose from death again;
For us he went on high to reign;
For us he sent his Spirit here
To guide, to strengthen, and to cheer.

All glory to our Lord and God
For love so deep, so high, so broad;
The Trinity whom we adore
Forever and forevermore.

Thomas a Kempis
Fifteenth century

FATHER, all-powerful and ever-living God,
we do well always and everywhere to give you
   thanks.

You celebrated your new gift of baptism
by signs and wonders at the Jordan.
Your voice was heard from heaven
to awaken faith in the presence among us
of the Word made [flesh].

Your Spirit was seen as a dove,
revealing Jesus as your servant,
and anointing him with joy as the Christ,
sent to bring to the poor
the good news of salvation.

Preface
Baptism of the Lord
Roman rite

THE Christian mysteries are an indivisible whole. If we become immersed in one, we are led to all the others. Thus the way from Bethlehem leads inevitably to Golgotha, from the crib to the cross. When the blessed virgin brought the child to the temple, Simeon prophesied that her soul would be pierced by a sword, that this child was set for the fall and the resurrection of many, for a sign that would be contradicted. His prophecy announced the passion, the fight between light and darkness that already showed itself before the crib.

Edith Stein

THE sun conquers
And the steps by which it approaches its zenith
Show forth a mystery.
Lo! It is twelve days since he began to mount upward
And today is the thirteenth day.
It is the perfect symbol of the Son and his twelve
        apostles.
The darkness of winter is conquered,
To show that Satan is conquered.
The sun conquers, so that all may know
That the only-begotten Son of God triumphs over all.

Ephraem the Syrian
Foruth century

Now, Master, you can dismiss your servant in peace;
   you have fulfilled your word.
For my eyes have witnessed your saving deed
      displayed for all the peoples to see:
A revealing light to the Gentiles,

Luke 2:29–32   the glory of your people Israel.

Notes

Winter Solstice

WE MUST SEE THE ENTIRE: *The Church's Year of Grace*, vol. 1, copyright © 1964 by the Order of St. Benedict, Inc. Published by The Liturgical Press, Collegeville MN. Used with permission.

HOW FAR CHRISTIANITY: *Christmas and Epiphany* by John Gunstone, © 1967 by The Faith Press.

THEY CALL: *The Liturgical Year* by Adrian Nocent. Copyright © 1977 by The Order of St. Benedict, Inc. Published by the Liturgical Press, Collegeville MN. Used with permission.

THE PEOPLE ARE: *The Liturgical Year* by Adrian Nocent. Copyright © 1977 by The Order of St. Benedict, Inc. Published by The Liturgical Press, Collegeville MN. Used with permission.

IN THE LITURGY: "Words at the Solstice: Four Theses and Eight Christmas Greetings" by Gordon Lathrop, *Dialog*, vol. 21, Fall 1982. Used by permission.

Christmas Eve

WE KNOW FROM OUR STUDY: from *The Christmas Tree Book* by Philip V. Snyder, copyright © 1976 by Philip Snyder. A Studio Book. Reprinted by permission of Viking Penguin Inc.

REJOICE, JERUSALEM: *Byzantine Daily Worship*, Joseph Raya/Jose de Vinck, © 1969. Reprinted with permission of Alleluia Press. All rights reserved.

THEY (THE COPTS) KEEP VIGIL: "The Celebration of the Christmas Cycle in the Eastern Churches" by Irenee-Henri Dalmais, from *Liturgy and Cultural Religious Traditions* (Concilium 102), ed. by Herman Schmidt and David Power, © 1977 by Stichting Concilium and the Seabury Press, Inc. Used by permission.

UNDERLYING ALL FESTIVE: *In Tune with the World* by Josef Pieper, trans. by Richard and Clara Winston, © 1973 by Franciscan Herald Press, 1434 West 51st St., Chicago IL 60609 Used by permission.

OF COURSE YOU: *Letters and Papers from Prison*, rev., enlarged ed. by Dietrich Bonhoeffer, © 1953, 1967, 1971 by SCM Press Ltd. Used by permission.

I HAVE LIGHTED THE CANDLES: Kenneth Patchen, *The Collected Poems of Kenneth Patchen* © 1942, 1957 by New Directions Publishing Corporation. Reprinted by permission.

IN RUSSIA, THE CUSTOM: *The Year of Grace of the Lord* by a Monk of the Eastern Church, © 1980 by St. Vladimir's Seminary Press, 575 Scarsdale Rd., Crestwood NY 10707. Used by permission.

IN TIME IT CAME ROUND: *The Poems of St. John of the Cross*, trans. by John Frederick Nims, © 1959 by John Frederick Nims. Reprinted by permission of The University of Chicago Press.

THE PRODIGIOUS EXPANSES: Specified excerpt (p. 76-77) from *Hymn of the Universe* by Pierre Teilhard de Chardin © 1961 by Editions du Feuil. English translation © 1965 by William Collins Sons & Company, Ltd. and Harper & Row Publishers, Inc. Reprinted by permission of Harper & Row Publishers, Inc.

IT IS TRULY: *The Writings of Edith Stein* trans. by Hilda Graef. Reprinted by permission of Paulist Press.

THE VIGIL OF CHRISTMAS: *The Church's Year of Grace*, vol. 1 by Pius Parsch. Copyright © 1959 by The Order of St. Benedict, Inc. Published by The Liturgical Press, Collegeville MN. Used with permission.

HAIL KING!: *Celtic Invocations* by Alexander Carmichael. Copyright © 1972 by Vineyard Books, Box 3315, Noroton CT 06820. Used by permission.

TODAY THE VIRGIN: *Byzantine Daily Worship*, Joseph Raya/Jose de Vinck, © 1969. Reprinted with permission of Alleluia Press. All rights reserved.

Christmas Midnight

WITHERED LEAVES PANIC: "Leaves in Solstice" by Dennis Kennedy, CM. Reprinted by permission of the author.

AT THAT TIME: *Byzantine Daily Worship*, Joseph Raya/Jose de Vinck, © 1969. Reprinted with permission of Alleluia Press. All rights reserved.

WHAT ADAM'S DISOBEDIENCE COST: *The Hymns and Ballads of Fred Pratt Green*. Copyright © 1978 by Hope Publishing Co., Carol Stream IL 60188. All rights reserved. Used by permission.

CHRISTMAS CALLS A COMMUNITY: *Liturgy*, vol. 1, no. 2, Copyright © 1980, The Liturgical Conference, 806 Rhode Island Ave. NE, Washinton DC 20018. All rights reserved. Used with permission.

THE BLESSED SON: "Hodie" by Ralph Vaughan Williams, text by Miles Coverdale after Martin Luther, © 1954 by Oxford University Press, used by permission.

YOU ARE HOLY: *Biblical Prayers* by Lucien Deiss. Copyright © 1976 by Rev. Lucien Deiss. Used with permission of World Library Publications.

THE WORD IS BORN: *The Hymns and Ballads of Fred Pratt Green.* Copyright © 1972 by Hope Publishing Co., Carol Stream IL 60188. All rights reserved. Used by permission.

I MEAN THE CENTRAL: *The Catholic Thing* by Rosemary Haughton, © 1979 by Rosemary Haughton, published by Templegate Publishers. Used by permission.

WIDE, WIDE IN THE ROSE'S SIDE: Kenneth Patchen, *The Collected Poems of Kenneth Patchen* © 1942, 1957 by New Directions Publishing Corporation. Reprinted by permission.

THOU WAST BORN: *Orthodox Hymns of Christmas, Holy Week and Easter* by Alexander Bogolepov, © 1965 by St. Vladimir's Seminary Press, 575 Scarsdale Rd., Crestwood NY 10707. Used by permission.

I WISH YOU COULD: "Joseph's Song" by Dennis Kennedy, CM. Reprinted by permission of the author.

O LORD, OUR GOD: *Selected Prayers* by Karl Barth, trans. by Keith R. Crim, © 1965 by M.E. Bratcher, published by John Knox Press. Used by permission.

Christmas Dawn

AT BETHLEHEM BORN: from *Early Christian Prayers,* ed. by A. Hamman, trans. by Walter Mitchell, published by Regnery Gateway, Inc. With permission.

MARY SPEAKS: *The Magnificat* by Sidney Callahan, © 1975 by The Seabury Press.

O MY CHILD: *Orthodox Hymns of Christmas, Holy Week and Easter* by Alexander Bogolepov, © 1965 by St. Vladimir's Seminary

Press, 575 Scarsdale Rd., Crestwood NY 10707. Used by permission.

TWAS IN THE MOON: *Canadian Hymnal*, #412. English text of the Huron Carol by J. E. Middleton. Used by permission of The Frederick Harris Music Co., Ltd.

WHOM HAVE YOU SEEN: *The Hours of the Divine Office in English and Latin*, vol. 1, copyright © 1963 by The Order of St. Benedict, Inc. Published by The Liturgical Press, Collegeville MN. Used with permission.

Christmas Day

LET US CELEBRATE: *The Liturgical Year* by Adrian Nocent. Copyright © 1977 by The Order of St. Benedict, Inc. Published by The Liturgical Press, Collegeville MN. Used with permission.

THIS DAY TRUE PEACE: *The Hours of the Divine Office in English and Latin*, vol. 1, copyright © 1963 by The Order of St. Benedict, Inc. Published by The Liturgical Press, Collegeville MN. Used with permission.

THE WHOLE CHURCH REJOICES: *Christmas and Epiphany* by John Gunstone, © 1967 by The Faith Press.

YOUR NATIVITY, O CHRIST: *Byzantine Daily Worship*, Joseph Raya/Jose de Vinck, © 1969. Reprinted with permission of Alleluia Press. All rights reserved.

WONDERFUL THE DIGNITY: from *Early Christian Prayers*, ed. by A. Hamman, trans. by Walter Mitchell, published by Regnery Gateway, Inc. With permission.

O GOD WHO MAKEST: *The Book of Common Prayer*, The Church Pension Fund, 800 Second Avenue, New York NY. Used by permission.

GRANT, WE PRAY YOU: from *Early Christian Prayers*, ed. by A. Hamman, trans. by Walter Mitchell, published by Regnery Gateway, Inc. With permission.

THE FATHER: *Christmas and Epiphany* by John Gunstone, © 1967 by The Faith Press.

CHRISTMAS 1970: "Words at the Solstice: Four Theses and Eight Christmas Greetings" by Gordon Lathrop, *Dialog*, vol. 21, Fall 1982. Used by permission.

LET ALL THE EARTH: *Prayers, Hymns and Anthems for the Byzantine Liturgy*, Rev. Austin P. Mohrbacher, Russian Center, Fordham University.

O SAVIOR OF OUR FALLEN RACE: *Lutheran Book of Worship*. Text copyright © 1978. Used by permission of Augsburg Publishing House.

THE RADIANCE: from *Early Christian Prayers*, ed. by A. Hamman, trans. by Walter Mitchell, published by Regnery Gateway, Inc. With permission.

A MARVELOUS CHANGE: from *Early Christian Prayers*, ed. by A. Hamman, trans. by Walter Mitchell, published by Regnery Gateway, Inc. With permission.

THY EPIPHANY, O LORD: *Christmas and Epiphany* by John Gunstone, © 1967 by The Faith Press.

CHRIST IS BORN. HE IS: *Seasons of Celebration* by Thomas Merton, © 1950, 1958, 1962, 1964, 1965 by the Abbey of Gethsemani. Reprinted by permission of Farrar, Straus and Giroux, Inc.

CHRIST IS BORN. GIVE HIM: *Byzantine Daily Worship*, Joseph Raya/Jose de Vinck, © 1969. Reprinted with permission of Alleluia Press. All rights reserved.

COME, THEN: *Sunday Sermons of the Fathers*, vol. 1, trans. and ed. by M.F. Toal, © 1957 by M.F. Toal, published by Longmans, Green & Co. Ltd.

TODAY THE DARKNESS: *The Liturgical Year* by Adrian Nocent. Copyright © 1977 by The Order of St. Benedict, Inc. Published by The Liturgical Press, Collegeville MN. Used with permission.

JESUS, SON OF THE LIVING GOD: *Praise God: Common Prayer at Taize* published by Oxford University Press, 200 Madison Ave., New York NY 10016.

O LORD, OUR GOD: *Selected Prayers* by Karl Barth, trans. by Keith R. Crim, © 1965 By M. E. Bratcher, published by John Knox Press. Used by permission.

HODIE CHRISTUS: *The Hours of the Divine Office in English and Latin*, vol. 1, copyright © 1963 by The Order of St. Benedict, Inc. Published by The Liturgical Press, Collegeville MN. Used with permission.

WE CAN KEEP ALL: *The Dynamics of Liturgy* by Hans A. Reinhold, © 1961 by Hans A. Reinhold and reprinted with permission of Macmillan Publishing Company.

Comites Christi

JUST AS IT IS: "Words at the Solstice: Four Theses and Eight Christmas Greetings" by Gordon Lathrop, *Dialog*, vol. 21, Fall 1982. Used by permission.

EVEN THE OLDEST: *The Liturgical Year* originally published in Germany as *Das Kirchenjahr mitfeiern* © 1979 Verlag Herder, English trans. © 1981 Pueblo Publishing Co., Inc. Used with permission.

A VOICE IS HEARD: *The Hours of the Divine Office in English and Latin*, vol. 1, copyright © 1963 by The Order of St. Benedict, Inc. Published by The Liturgical Press, Collegeville MN. Used with permission.

THE ECHO: *Kontakia of Romanos, Byzantine Melodist. I: On the Person of Christ*, trans. Marjorie Carpenter, by permission of the University of Missouri Press, © 1970 by the Curators of the University of Missouri.

THE TYRANT: from *Early Christian Prayers*, ed. by A. Hamman, trans. by Walter Mitchell, published by Regnery Gateway, Inc. With permission.

AS YET HEAVEN: *The Writings of Edith Stein* trans. by Hilda Graef. Reprinted by permission of Paulist Press.

WE REMEMBER TODAY: *Lesser Feasts and Fasts*. Copyright © 1980, The Church Hymnal Corporation, 800 Second Avenue, New York NY. Used by permission.

Holy Family

CHILD OF BETHLEHEM: "Christmas Prayer" by John Hammond, OSB from *Winter's Coming Home*, © 1975 by The Benedictine Foundation of the State of Vermont, Inc. Weston VT 05161.

LET US TOO STAND: from *Early Christian Prayers*, ed. by A. Hamman, trans. by Walter Mitchell, published by Regnery Gateway, Inc. With permission.

Mary, Mother of God

THE COMFORT: *The Magnificat* by Sidney Callahan, © 1975 by the Seabury Press.

HAIL MARY: from *Early Christian Prayers*, ed. by A. Hamman, trans. by Walter Mitchell, published by Regnery Gateway, Inc. With permission.

HAIL, O TRINITY: from *Early Christian Prayers*, ed. by A. Hamman, trans. by Walter Mitchell, published by Regnery Gateway, Inc. With permission.

ALL PEOPLE WHO HAVE: *The Magnificat* by Sidney Callahan, © 1975 by The Seabury Press.

IT IS INDEED RIGHT: from *Early Christian Prayers*, ed. by A. Hamman, trans. by Walter Mitchell, published by Regnery Gateway, Inc. With permission.

WHAT SHALL WE PRESENT: *Orthodox Hymns of Christmas, Holy Week and Easter* by Alexander Bogolepov, © 1965 by St. Vladimir's Seminary Press, 575 Scarsdale Rd., Crestwood NY 10707. Used by permission.

MARY WOVE A GARMENT: *The Liturgical Year* by Adrian Nocent. Copyright © 1977 by The Order of St. Benedict, Inc. Published by The Liturgical Press, Collegeville MN. Used with permission.

GRACE-FILLED: from *Early Christian Prayers*, ed. by A. Hamman, trans. by Walter Mitchell, published by Regnery Gateway, Inc. With permission.

THE BLESSING OF THE NEW YEAR: *Celtic Invocations* by Alexander Carmichael. Copyright © 1972 by Vineyard Books, Box 3315, Noroton CT 06820. Used by permission.

O LORD, OUR LOVING GOD: *Selected Prayers* by Karl Barth, trans. by Keith R. Crim, © 1965 by M.E. Bratcher, published by John Knox Press. Used by permission.

The Days of Christmas

O GOD, WHO DIDST: *The Book of Common Prayer*, The Church Pension Fund, 800 Second Avenue, New York NY. Used by permission.

Epiphany-Theophany

EGERIA, A NUN: *Christmas and Epiphany* by John Gunstone, © 1967 by The Faith Press.

THE EPIPHANY, HOWEVER: "The Celebration of the Christmas Cycle in the Eastern Churches" by Irenee-Henri Dalmais, from *Liturgy and Cultural Religious Traditions* (Concilium 102), ed. by Herman Schmidt and David Power, © 1977 by Stichting Concilium and The Seabury Press, Inc. Used by permission.

O GOD, WHO BY: *The Book of Common Prayer*, The Church Pension Fund, 800 Second Avenue, New York NY. Used by permission.

THE STAR WAS: *Christmas and Epiphany* by John Gunstone, © 1967 by The Faith Press.

ALMIGHTY GOD, WHOSE SON: *The Book of Common Prayer*, The Church Pension Fund, 800 Second Avenue, New York NY. Used by permission.

A STAR BURNED: *The Liturgical Year* by Adrian Nocent. Copyright © 1977 by The Order of St. Benedict, Inc. Published by The Liturgical Press, Collegeville MN. Used with permission.

ONLY A FEW: *Christmas and Epiphany* by John Gunstone, © 1967 The Faith Press.

THE GIFTS OF GOD: *The Liturgical Year* by Adrian Nocent. Copyright © 1977 by The Order of St. Benedict, Inc. Published by the Liturgical Press, Collegeville MN. Used with permission.

EXALTED KING: *Kontakia of Romanos, Byzantine Melodist. I: On the Person of Christ*, trans. Marjorie Carpenter, by permission of the University of Missouri Press, © 1970 by The Curators of the University of Missouri.

BEHOLD KINGS: *Sunday Sermons of the Fathers*, vol. 1, trans. and ed. by M.F. Toal, © 1957 by M.F. Toal, published by Longmans, Green & Co. Ltd.

MOST OF THE TRADITIONAL: *In Tune with the World* by Josef Pieper, trans. by Richard and Clara Winston, © 1973 by Franciscan Herald Press, 1434 West 51st St., Chicago IL 60609. Used by permission.

BY THIS THEY KNEW: "A Sermon for Epiphany" by Mark Searle, *Worship* 58:4. Copyright © 1984 by the Order of St. Benedict, Collegeville MN. All rights reserved.

BY BOWING: *The Liturgical Year* by Adrian

Nocent. Copyright © 1977 by the Order of St. Benedict, Inc. Published by the Liturgical Press, Collegeville MN. Used with permission.

THE LORD WENT: *The Liturgical Year* by Adrian Nocent. Copyright © 1977 by the Order of St. Benedict, Inc. Published by the Liturgical Press, Collegeville MN. Used with permission.

TODAY THOU HAST: *Kontakia of Romanos, Byzantine Melodist. I: On the Person of Christ,* trans. Marjorie Carpenter, by permission of the University of Missouri Press, © 1970 by the Curators of the University of Missouri.

ETERNAL GOD: *The Liturgical Year* by Adrian Nocent. Copyright © 1977 by The Order of St. Benedict, Inc. Published by The Liturgical Press, Collegeville MN. Used with permission.

THE BLESSING OF WATERS: *Christmas and Epiphany* by John Gunstone, © 1967 by The Faith Press.

ACCEPT FROM US: *The Liturgical Year* by Adrian Nocent. Copyright © 1977 by The Order of St. Benedict, Inc. Published by The Liturgical Press, Collegeville MN. Used with permission.

AT ST. PETERSBURG: *The Liturgical Year* by Adrian Nocent. Copyright © 1977 by The Order of St. Benedict, Inc. Published by The Liturgical Press, Collegeville MN. Used with permission.

IN THE FEAST FOREGONE: *Byzantine Daily Worship,* Joseph Raya/Jose de Vinick, © 1969. Reprinted with permission of Alleluia Press. All rights reserved.

GREAT IS THE LORD: *Family Festivals.* Reprinted with permission from Resource Publications, Inc., 160 E. Virginia St. #290, San Jose CA 95112.

INCLINE YOUR EAR: *Byzantine Daily Worship,* Joseph Raya/Jose de Vinick, © 1969. Reprinted with permission of Alleluia Press. All rights reserved.

BECAUSE THE LITURGY: *Christmas and Epiphany* by John Gunstone, © 1967 by The Faith Press.

THE HOLY DAY: *Christmas and Epiphany* by John Gunstone, © 1967 by The Faith Press.

WHAT GRACE WATER: *The Liturgical Year* by Adrian Nocent. Copyright © 1977 by The Order of St. Benedict, Inc. Published by The Liturgical Press, Collegeville MN. Used with permission.

HEROD, WHY: from *Early Christian Prayers,* ed.

by A. Hamman, trans. by Walter Mitchell, published by Regnery Gateway, Inc. With permission.

DEAR BROTHERS AND SISTERS: Epiphany proclamation trans. and adapted from the 1983 edition of the Italian Sacramentary, *Messale Romano,* by Peter Scagnelli.

Baptism of the Lord

FATHER IN HEAVEN, WHO: *The Book of Common Prayer,* The Church Pension Fund, 800 Second Avenue, New York NY. Used by permission.

WE ARE URGED TO MOVE: *Liturgy,* vol. 1, no. 2. Copyright 1980, The Liturgical Conference, 806 Rhode Island Ave. NE, Washington DC 20018. All rights reserved. Used with permission.

JESUS COMES OUT: *The Liturgical Year* by Adrian Nocent. Copyright © 1977 by The Order of St. Benedict, Inc. Published by The Liturgical Press, Collegeville MN. Used with permission.

Conclusion

THE CHRISTIAN MYSTERIES: *The Writings of Edith Stein* trans. by Hilda Graef. Reprinted by permission of Paulist Press.